RAND ARROYO CENTER

Russia and the West After the Ukrainian Crisis

European Vulnerabilities to Russian Pressures

F. Stephen Larrabee, Stephanie Pezard, Andrew Radin,
Nathan Chandler, Keith Crane, Thomas S. Szayna

Prepared for the United States Army

For more information on this publication, visit www.rand.org/t/RR1305

Library of Congress Cataloging-in-Publication Data is available for this publication.
ISBN: 978-0-8330-9306-6

Published by the RAND Corporation, Santa Monica, Calif.
© Copyright 2017 RAND Corporation
RAND® is a registered trademark.

Support RAND
Make a tax-deductible charitable contribution at
www.rand.org/giving/contribute

www.rand.org

Preface

This is the first in a series of reports on the impact and implications of the Ukraine crisis on European security. This paper examines European[1] vulnerabilities to various forms of possible Russian influence, pressure or coercion. For the purpose of this report, *vulnerability* is defined as a situation in which Russia has the capacity to exert political, economic, or military influence over European policy in ways that constrain European freedom of action and policy choices. Subsequent reports will examine Russian intentions and vulnerabilities, analyze possible reactions from the West to Russian policy, and recommend American and NATO policy responses.

The report should be of interest to those concerned with the impact on European security of Russia's annexation of Crimea and the potential leverage that Russia can further exert on several European countries. Primary research for this project was conducted from September 2014 to July 2015.

This research was sponsored by the Army Quadrennial Defense Review (QDR) Office in the Office of the Deputy Chief of Staff, G-8, Headquarters, Department of the Army, and was conducted within RAND Arroyo Center's Strategy, Doctrine, and Resources Program. RAND Arroyo Center, part of the RAND Corporation, is a feder-

---

[1] In this report, unless otherwise noted, we use *Europe* to mean the states of the European Union and NATO members other than the United States and Canada. In doing so, we do not seek to imply that other countries with all or some of their territory on the European continent (including Russia, Ukraine, Moldova, and Belarus) are not European.

ally funded research and development center sponsored by the United States Army.

The Project Unique Identification Code (PUIC) for the project that produced this document is HQD146843.

For comments or further information, please contact the project leader, James Dobbins (telephone 703-413-1100, extension 5099, email dobbins@rand.org).

For more information on RAND Arroyo Center, contact the Director of Operations (telephone 310-393-0411, extension 6419; fax 310-451-6952; email Marcy_Agmon@rand.org) or visit Arroyo's website at www.rand.org/ard/.

Table of Contents

Figures and Tables

Figures

Tables

Summary

Russia's illegal annexation of Crimea and effort to destabilize eastern Ukraine has forced the United States and its European allies to reassess their approach to Europe—a region once thought to be stable and secure. This report examines the vulnerabilities of the North Atlantic Treaty Organization (NATO) and European Union (EU) member states to Russian military and economic pressures and to Russian influence in their domestic politics. Subsequent reports will look at Russian capabilities and intentions, and recommend further possible U.S. and European actions.

Military Vulnerabilities

The annexation of Crimea and destabilization of eastern Ukraine have created a strong sense of insecurity and vulnerability among Russia's neighbors. The sense of vulnerability is particularly acute in the Baltic states (Estonia, Latvia, and Lithuania) because of their proximity to Russia and the large imbalance of military forces between Russia and the Baltic countries. Recent Russian behavior has exacerbated Baltic concerns. Since Vladimir Putin's return to the presidency, the number of border, airspace, and territorial waters violations has significantly increased. Russia also has conducted a range of large-scale exercises in the region, such as a snap-exercise in the Western Military District in March 2015 involving up to 38,000 troops, part of a substantial program of military exercises overall, including forces from its Western, Central, Eastern, and, to a lesser extent, Southern Military Districts.

This report analyzes four different types of military actions that Russia could take and their implications for Baltic security: (1) a large-scale short-notice action to seize all or large parts of the Baltic countries, (2) tactics mirroring those in eastern Ukraine designed to provoke an insurgency, (3) an effort to seize a small amount of territory with Russian-speaking majority population, and (4) limited and temporary incursions by Russian military personnel into Baltic airspace or territory. All of these are within Russian capabilities. Although Moscow's intentions are unclear, Russia's behavior in Crimea and eastern Ukraine creates an imperative for NATO to prepare for the possibility that Moscow may take military actions that would pose a serious threat to the sovereignty and independence of the Baltic states. It is unlikely that Russia could sustain control of Baltic territory, however, in the face of a likely NATO counteraction without threatening the use of nuclear weapons. In this connection, it is worth recalling that Europe and the United States remain vulnerable to Russian nuclear attack as Russia does to an American, French, and British nuclear attack. All of these countries rely on the threat of retaliation to deter such attack.

In the run-up to the NATO summit in Wales on September 4–5, 2014, the Polish and Baltic members argued that the annexation of Crimea and the effort to destabilize eastern Ukraine had fundamentally altered the existing security environment and made adjustments in NATO'S force posture essential. They pushed hard for NATO to permanently deploy combat troops on the soil of eastern member states. However, it proved impossible to achieve a consensus at the summit on permanently stationing combat troops on Polish and Baltic territory. Some members, particularly Germany, argued that permanent stationing of substantial troops on the territory of eastern members would be regarded as provocative by Russia. Instead, NATO has relied upon a "persistent" (as opposed to permanent) presence, provided by rotational forces.

However, there has been growing pressure, especially from Poland and the Baltic states, for the deployment of a permanent U.S. and/or NATO presence in their territory. At the NATO summit in July 2016, NATO leaders agreed to an "enhanced forward presence," including plans for the deployment on a continuous rotational basis of four multinational battalions, one in each of the three Baltic countries and Poland, and a "tailored forward presence" in southeastern Europe.[1] Though this decision represents a growth in forward presence, there will likely continue to be a gap between the desired and provided NATO presence on the Alliance's eastern flank.

Whether Alliance consensus will hold will heavily depend on Russian policy and actions. If Russia is seen by the Alliance to violate the Minsk II agreement signed by Russia, Ukraine, Germany, and France in early February 2015 or if Moscow takes other actions, such as supporting separatist attempts to expand their control of territory beyond that which they currently control, pressure could grow for NATO to reconsider the idea of permanently stationing combat troops on the soil of eastern Alliance members and take other actions, such as prepositioning of more stocks and equipment on the soil of eastern members of the Alliance. Moves of this sort do not require formal Alliance decision, although efforts will be made to maintain as broad a consensus as possible.

European governments do not presently seem greatly concerned about the growing disparity in substrategic nuclear/dual-use systems between NATO and Russia. This could change if the prospect of conflict with Russia in the Baltics, or elsewhere, becomes more immediate, perhaps leading European governments to urge countervailing American development and deployment of such systems, as they did in the 1980s.

Trade and Investment Vulnerabilities

Europe's vulnerability to disruptions in non-energy trade or in financial flows is even more limited. Only a very small share of the European Union's total nonenergy imports come from Russia. Except for a few commodities like titanium, European needs in almost all sectors can be readily covered by other suppliers. A small subset of European countries—Lithuania, Finland, Estonia, Poland, and Norway—has been disproportionately affected by Russian countersanctions on agri-

---

[1] See NATO, "Warsaw Summit Communique," July 9, 2016, Paragraph 40.

cultural, livestock, and fishery products when compared with other European countries, but these countries have also shown strong resolve in the face of Russian pressure. Advanced European economies, first and foremost Germany, have also suffered a slowdown in export-led growth in many nonagricultural industries, such as manufacturing, automobiles, chemicals, and machinery, because of the weakened Russian purchasing power and access to credit, but so far this has had limited impact on Germany's broader economy.

Pressure is growing among several European allies to lift the EU sanctions. However, to date the consensus has held. In January 2016, the European Union voted to maintain the sanctions until June 2016. Barring some significant concessions on Moscow's part, the sanctions are likely remain in place for the foreseeable future.

Energy Vulnerabilities

With regard to energy flows, Europe is less vulnerable to Russia than is generally perceived. Although Russia is by far the largest supplier of imported crude oil and refined oil products to the European Union, it is limited in its ability to threaten the EU member states with a cutoff. Because crude oil is traded on a global market, if Russia were to divert oil to other markets, global crude oil supplies would just be reshuffled, as crude oil pushed out by Russia in non-European markets would find its way to Europe. Some Central European refineries do depend on receiving Russian crude through the Druzhba pipeline, but Russia would have a difficult time diverting those supplies to other export markets because of capacity constraints at its oil export ports.

In the case of natural gas, a combination of increased imports of liquefied natural gas, greater use of alternative fuels, including coal, renewables, and fuel oil, electricity demand management, and reduction in industrial use of natural gas could serve to compensate for a total cutoff in imports of natural gas for the European Union as a whole. However, natural gas is where Russia can exert the most pressure on several of the smaller economies of northeastern and Central Europe that are heavily dependent on Russian supplies. Future development of gas terminals and, in the meantime, cooperative measures from the European Union could mitigate the effect of a potential Russian gas cutoff for these countries. It is also important to note that using energy supplies as leverage against European countries would be a costly tactic for Russia, whose economy relies to a considerable extent on the revenue generated by sales of natural gas.

Russia could also theoretically attempt to cut its connection to the electric power grid of the Baltic republics, which also connects to Belarus and Kaliningrad. However, it would have to first invest in integrating electric power distribution on its own territory to grids in other regions of Russia. Finally, Russia could potentially leverage offers of access to its large reserves of oil and natural gas to induce European energy companies to lobby their governments to adopt policies more favorable to Russia—but, as of 2015, such lobbying appeared still a long way from jeopardizing EU member states' unity on the sanctions policy toward Russia.

Political Vulnerabilities

A last source of vulnerability is related to European domestic politics. Russia could attempt to foster instability in a few countries, particularly Estonia and Latvia, which have large, disaffected Russian-speaking minorities. Further south, Greece and Cyprus face severe economic difficulties, and Hungary's leadership has shown some sympathy for Vladimir Putin. However, none of these countries is likely to risk challenging the European Union or NATO on an issue of such fundamental political importance as sanctions against Russia. These countries may complicate the decisionmaking process in NATO and the European Union, but they are not likely to be able to force a revision of the sanctions in the near future.

Another important concern is the rise of right-wing extremist parties in Europe—some of which, such as the National Front in France, have received open or tacit Russian support. Even short of actually entering government, these parties can influence their national debates, as the UK Independence Party was able to do in promoting British departure from the European Union. Actual assumption of governing power, for instance by the National Front in France, while not probable, has become a distinct possibility.

The situation warrants continued close monitoring as new vulnerabilities could appear, and small divergences may widen. European countries are at odds on how to respond to the Russian threat. Some, especially the Baltic states and Poland, argue for a robust response, including the deployment and permanent presence of combat forces on the territory of eastern members of the Alliance. Others, especially Italy, Spain, Greece, and Slovakia, want to see the sanctions against Russia lifted and favor a return to business as usual. Germany's role will be critical, and many NATO and EU members will be watching carefully to see what position Berlin takes. Thus, maintaining close ties and policy coordination with Berlin will be important. With other economic and security concerns competing for attention, some countries, such as Germany, are divided on how to respond to Russia's increasingly assertive behavior. At present, these divergences appear manageable. However, if they were to intensify, they could pose a serious obstacle to European and transatlantic unity.

Acknowledgments

The authors would like to thank Timothy Muchmore for initiating and supporting this project. We also thank David Ochmanek, Chris Chivvis, and Phil Gordon for their helpful comments. Other people also helped make this study possible. Our thanks go to Meagan Smith and Marlon Graf, who helped with the research; and to Thomas Browne for providing editing support. Any errors are solely our responsibility.

Abbreviations

EU	European Union
FDI	foreign direct investment
FPÖ	Freedom Party of Austria (Freiheitliche Partei Österreichs)
GDP	gross domestic product
INF	Intermediate-Range Nuclear Forces
LNG	liquefied natural gas
NATO	North Atlantic Treaty Organization
OIES	Oxford Institute of Energy Studies
PVV	Party for Freedom (Partij voor de Vrijheid, Netherlands)
UKIP	United Kingdom Independence Party
VJTF	Very High Readiness Joint Task Force (NATO)

CHAPTER ONE

Introduction

In the wake of Russia's annexation of Crimea and continued aggression in eastern Ukraine, the rest of Europe[1] has been forced to reassess its approach to a regional security environment previously thought to be stable and relatively benign. Does Russia now pose a threat to countries other than Ukraine and, if so, what is the nature of that threat? Russia cannot match the military strength of North Atlantic Treaty Organization (NATO) or the economic capacity of the European Union. However, these organizations depend heavily on unanimity among members to initiate combined action, meaning that their full potential may not always be mobilized.

This report analyzes the vulnerability of European states to various possible forms of Russian influence, pressure, and intimidation. For the purpose of this report, *vulnerability* is defined as a condition or set of conditions under which Russia has the capacity to exert political, economic, or military influence over European policy in ways that constrain European freedom of action and policy.

Four areas of European vulnerability are examined: military, trade and investment, energy, and political. In each of these areas we also look at steps that already have been taken or at least decided upon, to shore up identified weak points. Later reports will examine Russian capabilities and Russian vulnerabilities to counterpressures from the

---

[1] In this report, unless otherwise noted, we use *Europe* to mean the states of the European Union and NATO members other than the United States and Canada. In doing so, we do not seek to imply that other countries with all or some of their territory on the European continent (including Russia, Ukraine, Moldova, and Belarus) are not European.

West, as well as possible Russian intentions, and will suggest possible further Western responses to the more revisionist Russia that Europe now seems to face.

CHAPTER TWO

Military Vulnerabilities

The annexation of Crimea and attempt to destabilize eastern Ukraine have created a strong sense of insecurity and vulnerability in Eastern Europe. The sense of vulnerability is particularly acute in the Baltic states—Estonia, Latvia, and Lithuania—because of their proximity to Russia, the large imbalance of military forces between Russia and the Baltic states, and Russia's historical relationship to the region. Recent Russian behavior has exacerbated Baltic concerns. Since Putin's return to the presidency, the number of border, airspace, and territorial waters violations has significantly increased. Since mid-2013, NATO fighter planes policing Baltic airspace were scrambled more than 100 times—a tripling from 2013.[1] Latvia registered 150 "close incidents." Finland has had five violations of its airspace against a yearly average of one or two in the previous decade.[2] In many cases, the Russian pilots have turned off their transponders, making it impossible to communicate with the Russian aircraft. This is highly dangerous and increases the chances of an accident or a miscalculation that could lead to an inadvertent confrontation. Russia also has conducted a number of large-scale exercises in the region, such as a snap-exercise in the Western Military District in March 2015 involving up to 38,000 troops, part of a substantial pro-

---

[1]   Richard Milne, "Lithuania to Complete Western Integration as Kremlin Rattles Baltics," *Financial Times*, December 30, 2014b.

[2]   Richard Milne, Sam Jones, and Kathrin Hille, "Russian Air Incursions Rattle Baltic States," *Financial Times*, September 24, 2014.

gram of military exercises overall, including forces from its Western, Central, Eastern, and, to a lesser extent, Southern Military Districts.[3]

Russian Doctrine and Capabilities

Russia maintains a substantial strategic nuclear arsenal, capable of striking targets around the world, including in the United States. Russia, in turn, is vulnerable to U.S. strategic systems. Insofar as the threat of escalation to strategic nuclear strikes deters both sides from conflict with one another, these arsenals should preclude a strategic nuclear exchange, although Russian concerns (valid or not) that U.S. conventional capabilities, missile defense developments, and capacity to carry out a disarming first strike may make this standoff less stable than one might hope.[4]

At the substrategic level, both nuclear and conventional, the Intermediate-Range Nuclear Forces (INF) treaty bans ground-launched ballistic and cruise missiles (nuclear or conventional) with ranges from 500 to 5,500 km. A number of European countries are, of course, vulnerable to shorter-range Russian capabilities. Russia has been modernizing and expanding systems with lower ranges, including conventional surface-to-air capabilities and ballistic and cruise missiles. The newer Russian system that has arguably attracted the most attention is the 500-km range Iskander ballistic missile, whose capacity to carry nuclear warheads has been noted by Russian and Western commentators alike. Moscow is also developing cruise missiles of a variety of ranges that can be launched from a range of air- and sea-based

---

[3] Four of the exercises held between March 2013 and February 2015 involved more than 100,000 military personnel. Ian J. Brzezinski and Nicholas Varangis, "The NATO-Russia Exercise Gap," The Atlantic Council, February 23, 2015. This said, large snap-exercises are consistent with Russia's military behavior prior to the Ukraine conflict. See Bruce Jones, "Russia Places 38,000 Troops on Alert for Snap Exercises," *Jane's Defence Weekly*, March 16, 2015.

[4] See James T. Quinlivan and Olga Oliker, *Nuclear Deterrence in Europe: Russian Approaches to a New Environment and Implications for the United States,* Santa Monica, Calif.: RAND Corporation, MG-1075-AF, 2011.

platforms and which come in nuclear and conventional variants. These include the Kalibr (300–2,500-km range, nuclear and conventional capability), Kh-555 (3,500-km range), and Kh-101/2 (2,000–3,000-km range). Several analysts have speculated that a test of missiles developed for sea-based platforms (perhaps the Kalibr) from a land-based platform was what led to U.S. accusations of Russian noncompliance with the INF treaty.[5]

NATO countries also have short-range systems, of course, albeit not nuclear-capable ones deployed in theater (with the exception of gravity bombs for dual-capable aircraft). Thus, in this capability space, in the event of a conflict, Russia would have an advantage, which would need to be countered by other means. European governments do not at present seem greatly concerned about this imbalance, perhaps reassured by NATO's otherwise overwhelming conventional superiority, but they may become more worried in the future.

Russian military doctrine allows for the use of nuclear weapons only in the event of an existential threat to the state, not otherwise defined. Nonstrategic nuclear weapons are almost all in centralized storage, away from delivery vehicles, and it is difficult to mate nuclear weapons to their delivery systems even when they are co-deployed.[6] While Russia continues to invest in nuclear capabilities, particularly strategic capabilities, it has emphasized the development of better and more advanced conventional forces in recent years, and its newest doctrine speaks for the first time of "conventional deterrence."[7] All this said, the concern that the Russian nuclear threshold is lower than one might like remains. Not a few have speculated that Moscow's definition of an existential threat may be different from that of most Western states. Turn-of-the-century Russian writing regarding "de-escala-

---

[5] Nikolai N. Sokov, "Bill Gertz, New Russian SLCM, and the True Nature of Challenge to US and NATO," Arms Control Wonk Blog, August 25, 2015. See also Pavel Podvig, "Sorting Fact From Fiction on Russian Missile Claims," *Bulletin of the Atomic Scientists*, June 22, 2015.

[6] Igor Sutyagin, *Atomic Accounting: A New Estimate of Russia's Non-Strategic Nuclear Forces*, Occasional Paper, London: Royal United Services Institute, 2012.

[7] President of the Russian Federation, "Voennaia Doktrina Rossiiskoi Federatsii," December 26, 2015.

tory" nuclear strikes, combined with recent rhetoric by Russian leaders, have been cited by analysts in the West to argue that despite official doctrine, Russia could well intend to use nuclear weapons first and early in the event of conflict.[8] The rhetoric, particularly, raises concerns that plans and doctrine may not align perfectly, and the dual-capable nature of the Russian systems described above further increases the difficulty to anticipate and prepare for contingencies. Were the prospect of NATO conflict with Russia to become more immediate, and if Russian rhetoric indicates a real possibility of a lowered nuclear threshold, Europeans might become more concerned about this gap in the spectrum of deterrence, as they did in the 1980s in response to the Soviet build-up of intermediate range nuclear missiles.

Many European governments regard the chances of a Russian military attack on the Baltics as being very low. They argue that the risks outweigh any possible gains. Objectively speaking, this may be true. But Russian leaders may not see it that way. Moscow gave no warning of its actions in Crimea and eastern Ukraine; NATO faces the imperative to hedge against such low-probability but very high-risk scenarios. Moscow's calculus and future orientation are uncertain, and its recent behavior has raised tensions throughout the region.

Putin's leadership style is also important in this connection. Putin is a risk-taker. He has been successful in large part because he has been ready to do the unexpected. The annexation of Crimea provides a prominent example. The annexation caught Western leaders by surprise, leaving them flatfooted and unable—especially in the case of the Ukrainian government—to take effective countervailing military measures. Militarily, the annexation was a remarkable success. It was smoothly and efficiently executed without firing a shot. Indeed, Putin seems to have been surprised at the ease with which the annexation was

---

[8]   On "de-escalation," see Quinlivan and Oliker, 2011, and Nikolai N. Sokov, "Why Russia Calls a Limited Nuclear Strike 'De-escalation,'" *Bulletin of the Atomic Scientists*, March 13, 2014. For an assertion that Russian doctrine incorporates "de-escalation," see Elbridge Colby, *Nuclear Weapons in the Third Offset Strategy: Avoiding a Nuclear Blind Spot in the Pentagon's New Initiative,* Washington, D.C.: Center for a New American Security, January 2015.

accomplished, and it may have emboldened him to think the success could be replicated elsewhere.

When challenged, Putin's inclination, as evidenced over the last year and a half, seems to be to double down and raise the ante, as he did in the wake of the shooting down of the Malaysian commercial airliner MH17 in July 2014. Instead of seeking to defuse the crisis in the face of worldwide condemnation of Russia's behavior, he escalated the conflict, increasing military support for the separatists in eastern Ukraine and sending several thousand well-armed and well-trained Russian regular army soldiers clandestinely into Ukraine. This bold move shifted the tide of battle in the separatists' favor and resulted in a serious setback for the Ukrainian forces.

Possible Scenarios in the Baltics

The Baltic states in particular feel a strong sense of insecurity and vulnerability. The existing military balance, geography, and demography—as well as recent Russian behavior in the three Baltic states—make the current leaders of the Baltic states concerned about potential Russian aggression against their territory. This could occur in various forms. Next, we analyze four possible scenarios of military actions that Russia could take and their implications for Baltic security: (1) a large-scale short-notice action to seize all or large parts of the Baltic countries, (2) tactics mirroring those in eastern Ukraine designed to provoke an insurgency, (3) an effort to seize a small amount of territory with Russian-speaking majority population (for instance, Narva in Estonia or Daugavpils in Latvia), or (4) limited and temporary incursions by Russian military personnel into Baltic airspace or territory.

Russia possesses substantial major military superiority over the Baltic countries. Estonia and Latvia are small countries—1.3 and 2 million respectively (Lithuania has a population of nearly 3 million)—with small militaries that have only light capabilities.[9] By contrast, Russian

---

[9]   International Institute for Strategic Studies, "Military Balance 2015," Chapters 4 and 5, February 2015.

military capabilities in the Western Military District alone are significant—ongoing RAND open source research estimates that depending on how events in Ukraine develop, Russia could deploy 40 to 50 Battalion Task Groups (BTGs) to fight in the Baltics, backed by substantial air and missile assets.

A large-scale short-notice Russian invasion could reach the capitals of Estonia, Latvia, and, with greater difficulty, Lithuania within a few days.[10] NATO today has only small, company-sized ground force units rotationally deployed in the Baltics, and its rapidly deployable ground forces are light and could be bypassed or defeated by Russian forces. NATO could deploy substantial numbers of combat aircraft to the region on short notice, but these forces would have to cope with dense, modern Russian air defenses and thus would probably be unable to heavily damage invading Russian forces early in a conflict. NATO does retain overall conventional superiority, and, given several months to deploy American and European armored forces, as well as artillery and extensive combat support assets, NATO would probably be able to eject Russian forces in a conventional counteroffensive. But this would cost thousands of lives and would run the risk that Russia might threaten to use nuclear weapons if it found itself facing a possible military defeat.

The second lower-intensity scenario involves an attempt by Russia to encourage an insurgency mirroring the ongoing insurgency by the separatists in eastern Ukraine. In this scenario, Russia would seek to use the discontent of Russian speakers in the Baltic countries as a pretext for military intervention. Russian-speaking minorities constitute approximately 25 percent of the population in Estonia and 27 percent in Latvia. As discussed in greater detail in the political section of this report, many Russian speakers in both countries are poorly integrated into Baltic political life and institutions and feel that they are treated

---

[10] See also David A. Shlapak and Michael W. Johnson, *Reinforcing Deterrence on NATO's Eastern Flank: Wargaming the Defense of the Baltics*, Santa Monica, Calif.: RAND Corporation, RR-1253-A, 2016.

as second-class citizens.[11] Russia could attempt to encourage the development of a separatist movement among Russians and Russian speakers in Estonia and Latvia using the same irregular tactics it used in eastern Ukraine, such as strategic ambiguity, deception, propaganda and manipulation of the media, cyberattacks, and covert actions to create or support violent and nonviolent opposition.[12] However, the socioeconomic environment for employing such tactics is far less fertile in the Baltics than in Ukraine. One report based on survey research in Latvia, for example, suggests that though there are large groups in the country that support Russia's narratives, "the possibility of mass protests and broad, active support for provocations started by Russia [is] unlikely."[13] Even in eastern Ukraine, it is not clear that these activities, other than covert actions, were particularly decisive. Therefore, Moscow would have a much more difficult time organizing a serious insurgency in Estonia and Latvia than was the case in eastern Ukraine.

Instead of seeking to develop a large-scale insurgency, Russia could seize a small amount of Estonian or Latvian territory populated by a Russian majority. Allegations of the poor treatment of the Russian population could be used as a pretext to justify Russian military action with the stated goals of protecting the Russian population and demonstrating the failure of NATO to defend the entire territory of the Baltic countries. We already have judged outright invasion militarily plausible, so this scenario is also within Russia's capabilities. However, for the same reasons, even a small land grab would prove challenging, as Russia would then be faced with defending a small enclave

---

[11] On Estonia, for example, see Juhan Kivirähk, "Integrating Estonia's Russian-Speaking Population: Findings Findings of National Defense Opinion Surveys," International Centre for Defense and Security, December 2014.

[12] These tactics are often collectively referred to as *hybrid*—see, for example, Milne 2014(b), as well as Edgar Buckley and Ioan Pascu, "NATO's Article 5 and Russian Hybrid Warfare," March 17, 2015; and Peter Pindják "Deterring Hybrid Warfare: A Chance for NATO and the EU to Work Together?" *NATO Review*, 2014.

[13] Survey research conducted in Latvia supports this assessment. See Ieva Berzina, ed., "The Possibility of Societal Destabilization in Latvia: Potential National Security Threats, Executive Summary of the Research Report," Riga, Latvia, Center for Security and Strategic Research, National Defence Academy of Latvia, 2016, pp. 29–30.

against a delayed but substantially reinforced NATO response. The risk of nuclear escalation if Russia seemed on the verge of being defeated would also be present.

Finally, Russia could continue to engage in violations of air and sea space and other similar provocations. These incidents are designed to test Western resolve and remind the Baltic leaders of their vulnerability. Their basic goal is to undermine confidence in NATO's Article 5 security guarantee and to raise doubts in the minds of Baltic leaders regarding the willingness of NATO to honor its commitment to defend the Baltic states in case of a threat to their security.

Several issues complicate the attempt to devise a countervailing strategy that can successfully deter potential threats to the sovereignty and security of the Baltic states. The first is the existence of the Russian minority. Estonia and Latvia have large ethnic Russian minorities on their territory. Close to 25 percent of their population are ethnic Russians. The geographical distribution of the politically unintegrated Russian minority is an additional potential source of vulnerability because many Russophones are concentrated in areas bordering directly on Russia—namely, Ida-Virumaa in Estonia and Latgale in Latvia. The existence of these minorities provides a ready-made instrument for exerting pressure on the two Baltic states, especially because Putin has stressed Russia's responsibility to protect the welfare of ethnic Russians and Russian speakers living outside Russia's borders. Russia could use the alleged mistreatment of the Russian minority in Estonia or Latvia as a pretext for taking military action against one or both countries.

Given the risks associated with an overt military attack on one or more Baltic states, Russia might choose to utilize a combination of deception, clandestine subversion and sabotage, and strategic ambiguity to intimidate the Baltic states and weaken their sovereignty. The ambiguous nature of the threat could make it difficult for the Alliance to come to a consensus about how to respond. A long delay in coming to agreement on a response could have a very damaging psychological impact, deepening doubt and mistrust about the credibility of NATO's security guarantee (Article 5). Brookings scholar Steven Pifer has argued that, "If 100 little green men seize a government building in Estonia and NATO spends weeks debating whether this is an Article 5 contingency, Putin will have won big."[14] This may not necessarily be true (particularly if the little green men go no further), but it does represent a challenge. Of course, the United States and other key allies would remain free to respond to such a challenge without a formal NATO decision if they so choose.

Russian efforts to use unconventional approaches and conduct a mixture of regular and irregular warfare raise important issues for NATO and national planners. These include questions such as, "When does Article 5 apply?" "What is the threshold and how can it be identified before that threshold is crossed?" "What actions can be taken before the North Atlantic Council (NAC) has formally authorized a response by NATO?" and "What might trigger national decision with or without a NATO consensus?"

Sweden and Finland

Russian actions in Ukraine have intensified Sweden's and Finland's interest in closer cooperation with NATO and have given the debate regarding possible Swedish and Finnish membership in NATO new impetus. Although neither country is likely to join NATO in the next few years, both governments have stepped up defense cooperation with the Alliance recently.[15] Finland and Sweden are increasingly important to NATO's defense planning.[16] Both signed host nation support agreements with NATO at the Wales summit in early September 2014, indicating the readiness under some circumstances to receive assistance from allied forces and allow NATO to use their military assets, such as ships and aircraft.

---

[14] Steven Pifer, "NATO's Response Must Be Conventional Not Nuclear," *Survival*, Vol. 57, No. 2, April–May 2015, p. 120.

[15] For a detailed discussion, see F. Stephen Larrabee, Peter A. Wilson, and John Gordon IV, *The Ukrainian Crisis and European Security*, Santa Monica, Calif.: RAND Corporation, RR-903-A, 2015, pp. 36–37.

[16] Andrew A. Michta, "Putin Targets the Scandinavians," *American Interest*, November 17, 2014.

Recently, Moscow has stepped up efforts to undo the budding cooperation between Sweden, Finland, and NATO and ultimately to neutralize the two countries through direct and indirect military, economic, and political means. Moscow's goal is to force the two Nordic states to opt out of any confrontation with Russia and prevent NATO from using Swedish air space and territory. Russian planning, exercises, and patterns of harassment seek to convey to Sweden and Finland that if Russia should so choose, it could also target their territories.[17]

U.S. and European Responses

Since the start of the Ukraine crisis, the United States and its European allies have taken a number of steps to try to mitigate real and perceived vulnerabilities to Russian military pressure and possible aggression in Europe. In the immediate aftermath of the Russian annexation of Crimea, the United States deployed 12 F-15s and F-16s to Poland to assist in air operations there and augmented the U.S. naval presence in the Baltic Sea.[18] While these moves were welcomed by Poland and the three Baltic states, they were viewed as insufficient. In the discussions leading up to the NATO summit in Wales in 2014, Polish officials pushed for the permanent deployment of two heavy brigades—about 10,000 soldiers—on Polish soil.[19] The Baltic states also let it be known that they would welcome the deployment of American troops on their soil.

---

[17] Michta, 2014.

[18] U.S. Navy vessels have routinely been deployed to the Baltic Sea as part of Operation Atlantic Resolve since early 2014. See U.S. European Command, "Operation Atlantic Resolve (2014)," fact sheet, 2014; and U.S. Department of Defense, "America's Continued Commitment to European Security: Operation Atlantic Resolve," web page, undated. Since 1971, NATO has also carried out an annual U.S.-led exercise in the Baltic Sea (BALTOPS). See NATO, "NATO Allies Begin Naval Exercise BALTOPS in the Baltic Sea," website, June 20, 2015.

[19] Neil Buckley, James Fontanella-Khan, and Jan Cienski, "Poland Calls for NATO Troop Deployment," *Financial Times*, April 1, 2014.

At this summit, Poland and the Baltic states pressed hard for the permanent stationing of NATO troops on the territory of the eastern members of the Alliance. They argued that the annexation of Crimea and the attempt by Russia to destabilize eastern Ukraine had fundamentally altered the security environment in Europe, and that NATO should no longer be bound by the commitment contained in the NATO-Russia Founding Act not to station substantial NATO combat troops on the territory of the new members in Eastern Europe.[20] However, it proved impossible to obtain a consensus for the permanent stationing of NATO troops on the territory of the new eastern members of the Alliance because Germany and several other Alliance members opposed the proposal for deploying troops permanently in Eastern Europe, arguing that Russia would regard such a move as provocative. Instead, the leaders of NATO decided to increase the number of troops stationed on the soil of the eastern member states on a rotational basis. The United States also reiterated NATO's security guarantee. During a stopover in Estonia en route to the Wales summit, President Barack Obama reaffirmed the NATO commitment to ensure the sovereignty and independence of the three Baltic states, stating that, "Today we are bound by our treaty Alliance . . . . You lost your independence once before. With NATO, you will never lose it again."[21]

To underscore the seriousness of the U.S. commitment, Obama launched the European Reassurance Initiative (ERI), a $1 billion effort that includes increased rotational deployments of U.S. forces to the Baltics and additional security assistance to include upgrading military infrastructure.[22] On a rotational basis, the U.S. Army has deployed approximately a battalion of troops to the three Baltic countries from units including the 173rd Airborne, 1st Cavalry Division, 4th Infantry

---

[20] For a detailed discussion, see Mark Kramer, "The New Russian Chill in the Baltic," *Current History, Current History*, Vol. 114, No. 770, March 2015, pp. 108–114.

[21] The White House, Office of the Press Secretary, "Remarks by President Obama to the People of Estonia," speech in Tallinn, Estonia, September 3, 2014. See also comments by German Chancellor Angela Merkel in "Merkel Pledges NATO Will Defend Baltic Member States," *Reuters*, August 18, 2014.

[22] See U.S. Department of Defense, "America's Continued Commitment to European Security: Operation Atlantic Resolve," web page, undated.

Division, and 2nd Cavalry Regiment.[23] These forces train with their host-nation counterparts. If Russian forces were to attack one or more Baltic states, U.S. ground forces there could act as a "trip wire," underscoring the U.S. commitment to defend treaty allies.[24]

At the Wales summit, NATO took a number of other important steps designed to enhance its ability to deter threats to the Baltic states. Of particular importance was the decision to create a Readiness Action Plan, which included the development of a 5,000-troop Very High Readiness Joint Task Force (VJTF) capable of deploying within one to five days.[25] Two other important steps followed some months later. In June 2015, while on a trip to Europe, Secretary of Defense Ashton Carter announced that the United States would contribute special operations forces, weapons, and surveillance aircraft to NATO's VJTFs.[26] The following day in Tallinn, he stated that the United States would preposition 250 tanks, armored vehicles, and artillery across several Central and East European countries, including Bulgaria, Estonia, Latvia, Lithuania, Poland, and Romania. These moves are designed to enhance the ability of NATO to react quickly to any Russian threat to the security of the eastern members of the Alliance, particularly the Baltic states. News reports suggest that the United States is considering the further prepositioning of heavy combat equipment in Eastern Europe.

At the Warsaw Summit in July 2016, NATO expanded its plans for forward presence as part of an explicit strategy of deterrence. To implement this strategy, NATO leaders agreed to an "enhanced forward presence," including the deployment on a continuous rotational

---

[23] See U.S. European Command, 2014; U.S. Department of Defense, undated; Cheryl Pellerin, "U.S. Troops Resuming Atlantic Resolve Training in Eastern Europe," DoD News, January 12, 2015.

[24] Philip M. Breedlove, "Transcript: After the Summit: General Philip M. Breedlove on NATO's Path Forward," Washington, D.C., Atlantic Council, September 19, 2014; Olga Oliker, Michael McNearney, and Lynn Davis, *NATO Needs a Comprehensive Strategy for Russia*, Santa Monica, Calif.: RAND Corporation, PE-143-OSD, 2015.

[25] NATO, "NATO's Readiness Action Plan," fact sheet, December 2014.

[26] Geoff Dyer, "Carter Confirms Heavy Arms for Europe in Face of Russian Threat," *Financial Times,* June 24, 2015.

basis beginning in 2017 of four multinational battalions, one in each of the three Baltic countries and Poland, and a "tailored forward presence" in southeastern Europe including the development of a framework training brigade.[27] Though this decision represents a growth in forward presence, there will likely continue to be a gap between the desired and provided NATO presence on the Alliance's eastern flank.

Conclusion

There has been consensus among key NATO governments—including the United States—in favor of increased rotations of troops on the territory of Eastern European members rather than establishing a permanent military presence. Whether this consensus will hold will heavily depend on Russian behavior. If Russia is seen by the Alliance to violate the Minsk II agreement signed by Russia, Ukraine, Germany, and France in early February 2015, or if Moscow takes other actions, such as supporting separatist attempts to expand their control of territory beyond that which they currently control, pressure could grow to reconsider the option of permanently stationing combat troops on the soil of eastern Alliance members.

Finally, while NATO requires unanimity among its members to act as an alliance, the decision to send, to receive, and to employ forces is preeminently a national prerogative that need not depend on Alliance-wide concurrence. In the event of a mounting crisis, these decisions will be reached in London, Paris, Berlin, Warsaw, and, above all, Washington and may be executed whether or not every member of NATO agrees.

---

[27] See NATO, 2016, Paragraph 40.

CHAPTER THREE

Trade and Financial Vulnerabilities

Countries with close economic ties can face substantial economic costs if those ties are broken. Governments use sanctions and other economic policy measures that might break or attenuate these ties, or use threats to take such measures, as means to seek change in policies in countries with which they are in dispute. Governments also use economic inducements in attempts to affect policies in the targeted country.

The vulnerability of a country to these economic pressures or inducements to change its policies is affected by the extent of these ties, alternative export markets, sources of imports, or sources of finance, and the economic health of the country. Countries like Greece, facing deep economic problems, are less able to ignore economic pressures from other countries than countries where economic conditions are better.

Economic linkages between Europe and Russia therefore represent another realm in which Moscow may exercise leverage. Hostile Russian actions could include keeping the current trade embargo on imports of foodstuffs in place to reduce exports from the European Union to Russia; extending the sanctions to other sectors, including other agricultural and food products not currently covered; and abrogating contracts in the defense and dual-use sectors. Russia could also expropriate financial and other assets owned by European or North American companies or citizens, refuse to pay creditors from these countries, or otherwise disrupt financial markets. It could also provide financial support to European Union (EU) or NATO member states, such as Cyprus or Greece, undergoing financial difficulties.

In this section, we focus on European vulnerabilities to further disruptions in trade with Russia. We also investigate the potential for financial disruptions to these countries stemming from Russia by looking at stocks and flows of assets and liabilities. As part of this assessment, we also look at the extent to which the current sanctions and countersanctions regimes impose economic costs on EU and NATO member states. These assessments are intended to assist U.S. policymakers in gauging potential European reluctance to maintain or extend Western sanctions on Russia in the future. This chapter concludes that although Western European politicians could face pressure from domestic banks, oil companies, and defense contractors to lift the sanctions against Russia and normalize trade relations, because Russia does not account for very large shares of export sales from EU member states, overall, Moscow's ability to exert leverage on these states through bans on imports is limited. Furthermore, anything the Russians could do to inflict economic costs on EU member states through bans on imported goods from those countries would also hurt the Russian economy and consumers.

Foreign Trade

A country's vulnerability to a reduction in trade is commensurate with the extent to which it trades with another country and the ease with which it can shift exports to other markets or import from other suppliers. In this section, we use trade statistics to assess the extent of trade between European states and Russia in an effort to evaluate the vulnerability of these countries to further disruptions in trade with Russia.

In 2013, only about 1 percent of the European Union's total nonenergy imports came from Russia. Most of these imports, such as steel and chemicals, could be purchased from other suppliers. The main exception is titanium, where Russia is the primary producer. The few EU member states that still operate aging Soviet military equipment would have difficulty obtaining replacement parts for these weapons from sources other than Russia. All other nonenergy imports from Russia are readily available from other global markets.[1]

Russia has been an important market in some product areas for EU member states. Russia's countersanctions on exports of European agricultural, livestock, and fishery products have had substantial effects on some EU agricultural exporters.[2] In 2013, the 29 European economies facing countersanctions exported about $9 billion worth of goods now on Russia's list of embargoed products. These exports represented about 5.6 percent of total EU exports to Russia, but only 0.2 percent of EU total exports globally. Industry groups in several European states—including Italy, Greece, Hungary, Spain, Cyprus, Slovakia, and Austria[3]—have come out publicly against continued EU sanctions on Russia, arguing that Russia would respond to an end to EU sanctions by ending its own countersanctions. In 2013, as shown in Figure 3.1, the agricultural, livestock, and fishery commodities embargoed under Russia's countersanctions regime accounted for at least 10 percent of exports to Russia from eight European economies: Norway (76 percent), Cyprus (51 percent), Greece (32 percent), Denmark (28 percent), Ireland (25 percent), Lithuania (22 percent), Spain (14 percent), and Poland (10 percent).

However, in all but a few cases, when these national baskets of embargoed exports are viewed in the context of each country's share of total exports (on the embargo list) to all world markets—rather than in shares of total exports to Russia—a much different picture emerges (see Figure 3.1). For instance, in 2013, Norway exported to Russia $1.1 billion in goods that are now on the embargo list—primarily fish—equaling 76 percent of total Norwegian exports to Russia. But

---

[1] In 2013, the EU28 imported about 3.7 trillion euros in nonenergy goods, of which only 46.3 billion euros were imports from Russia. This 46.3 billion euros of nonenergy imports represented 22 percent of all Russian goods traded to the European Union. Source: Eurostat, undated, Comext Database.

[2] In August 2014, Russia imposed a one-year ban on imports of beef, pork, fish, fruit, vegetables, cheese, milk, and other dairy products from the European Union, Norway, the United States, Canada, and Australia.

[3] See, for instance, James Neuger, "Is EU Support for Russia Sanctions Waning? See Who's Visiting the Kremlin," *Bloomberg Business*, March 17, 2015.

Figure 3.1
Embargoed Goods Exported to Russia, as Share of All Exports to Russia and as a Share of Exports by All Countries of Products on the Sanctions List in 2013

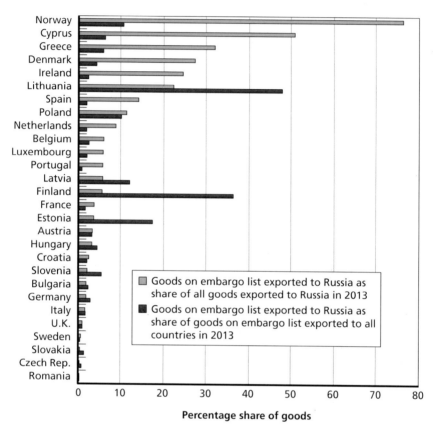

SOURCE: UN Comtrade Database, RAND calculations.
RAND RR1305-3.1

Norway exported an additional $9.3 billion in goods covered under the embargo list to the rest of the world in 2013. This means that the Russian market constituted only 11 percent of Norwegian sales of fish and other agricultural products. Viewed in this light, the Russian sanctions appear far less threatening to the Norwegian economy; the Norwegian fishery industry is not highly dependent on Russian markets. Indeed, as shown in Figure 3.1, Russian consumers constituted at least 10 percent of market share for only five European states' total exports of agricultural, livestock, and fishery goods affected by the embargo: Lithuania, Finland, Estonia, Norway, and Latvia. Yet these countries have been among those most supportive of keeping EU sanctions in place, suggesting that they can—or are at least ready to—bear the economic costs of reduced exports to Russia.[4]

It is also important to note that some amount of European embargoed goods still makes its way to Russia via third countries. Russian authorities seem to have somewhat cut the flow of goods from Belarus and Kazakhstan, but other countries could replace these two countries as platforms for re-exports of banned European agricultural products in the future.[5]

Even if Russia had not imposed countersanctions on agricultural imports from the European Union and North America, exports of these products to Russia still would likely have declined. Looking at exports of nonembargoed products, we find exports to Russia of many have fallen sharply because of the steep declines in the purchasing power of Russian consumers due to the weakened ruble. The decline in the value of the ruble has been due to reductions in Russian export revenues driven by plummeting oil prices, borrowing restrictions imposed on Russian banks under Western sanctions, and private capital flight from Russians. The ruble also has fallen because foreign investors have sought to limit or offload their financial exposure to Russia to avoid increased risks associated with the declining Russian economy and Putin's policies. Demand for imports, especially consumer durables and investment goods, have fallen because of higher domestic interest rates. As a result of weakened Russian purchasing power and access to credit, many European economies are suffering a slowdown in exports in many nonagricultural industries such as manufacturing, automobiles, chemicals, and machinery. For instance, in the first half of 2014, German auto manufacturer Daimler saw a 20-percent increase in Russian business, but then its sales of cars and trucks fell due to declin-

[4] Neuger, 2015.

[5] Kenneth Rapoza, "Here's What Putin's Counter-Sanctions Did To EU Exporters," *Forbes*, April 17, 2015.

ing oil prices and the economic consequences of the Ukraine crisis.[6] Overall, exports of German motor vehicles and automotive parts to Russia fell 27 percent in the first eight months of 2014, while exports of machinery declined by 17 percent.[7] These declines in exports have hurt overall sales of EU businesses for which Russia has been an important market. A number of German business ventures in Russia have already been downsized or put on hold. In December 2014, German chemical company BASF canceled a gas extraction and distribution project with Gazprom.[8] The German Russian Chamber of Commerce found that 41 percent of German companies operating in Russia already have slowed their investment in the country. More than a third plans on canceling some of their planned investments.[9]

EU-imposed sanctions and rising political tensions also threaten to have a direct impact on exports by stalling or abrogating large contracts in the defense and dual-use technology sectors. To date, however, there have been only a handful of such cases—the most high-profile of which was the cancellation of France's delivery of two Mistral-class amphibious assault ships to Russia. In August 2014, Germany's Federal Ministry of Economics blocked defense and automotive manufacturer Rheinmetall's $134 million contract to construct a modern military training/combat simulation center in Russia because of increasing financial and political risk. In April 2014, Sweden's Volvo announced it would delay plans to partner with Russian tank manufacturer Uralvagonzavod OAO to build armored personnel carriers, citing the "uncertainty factor" following Russia's annexation of Crimea.[10]

---

[6] "Ukraine Crisis Hampers German Carmaker's Russia Growth," *Moscow Times*, August 3, 2014.

[7] Friedrich Geiger, "German Exports to Russia Fall off Further as Sanctions Take Hold: New Data Shows Sharp Decline," *Wall Street Journal*, October 29, 2014.

[8] Leonhard Foeger, "Gazprom, BASF Abandon Multibillion Dollar Asset Swap," *Reuters*, December 19, 2014.

[9] Based on a survey of 200 German firms with operations in Russia, cited in Jack Ewing and Alison Smale, "In Reversal, Germany Cools to Russian Investment," *New York Times*, December 28, 2014.

[10] Christina Zander and John D. Stoll, "Volvo Trucks Put Russian Tank Deal on Ice," *Wall Street Journal*, April 8, 2014.

Foreign Direct and Portfolio Investment

Some EU member states could be vulnerable to a reduction of capital flows from Russia into their economies. EU investors and banks could be vulnerable to write-offs of investments in Russia because of Russian government policies or indirectly through bankruptcies of Russian borrowers.

Officially, Cyprus is overwhelmingly the largest source and destination of Russian foreign direct investment (FDI), though these figures belie the round-tripping in which Russians engage. Cyprus has been a tax haven for Russian individuals and firms. Most of the Russian financial flows to and from Cyprus are channeled through Russian-owned Cypriot shell corporations. Cyprus's growing economic and strong financial ties to Russia have raised concerns in Brussels. Many EU officials fear that these ties could give Moscow a potential means of influencing Cypriot policy, particularly regarding future contracts for the natural gas reserves currently under exploration off the Cypriot coast.[11]

These concerns have been reinforced by the Republic of Cyprus's growing economic problems. Cyprus has the second-highest private indebtedness as a share of GDP in the Eurozone and the European Union.[12] The country has remained solvent because of a 10 billion–euro rescue package from the European Central Bank, the European Union, and the International Monetary Fund (IMF). Russia also has chipped in with a 2.5 billion–euro loan in 2011, extended under more favorable terms in 2013.[13] Putin has since wooed Cyprus in an effort to break the EU consensus on sanctions. So far, Cyprus has voted to maintain the sanctions, but pressure for a rupture is mounting, and

---

[11] Christopher Coats, "Where Does the Cyprus Deal Leave Its Natural Gas?" *Forbes*, March 28, 2013; Max Fisher, "A Bailout for Cyprus, a Geopolitical Failure for Russia," *Washington Post,* March 25, 2013.

[12] "A Fifth Bitter Lemon," *Economist,* June 30, 2012.

[13] Dan Bilefsky, "Cyprus Weighs Russian Loan or a Bailout from Europe," *New York Times,* June 14, 2012; "Russia Agreed to Restructure Bailout Loan to Cyprus, Putin Says," *Bloomberg Business,* April 8, 2013; Andreas Hadjipapas, "Cyprus Nears €2.5bn Russian Loan Deal," *Financial Times,* September 14, 2011.

President Nicos Anastasiades has expressed grave doubts about the wisdom of the sanctions. In February 2015, Moscow approved a second restructuring of the 2.5 billion–euro loan, lowering the interest rate and extending its maturity, and in exchange for Moscow's continued debt relief, Cyprus agreed to allow Russian naval ships access to its ports for resupply and maintenance.[14]

Following Cyprus, Russia's most important FDI and portfolio investment partners are all located in Western Europe (Figure 3.2). Overall, Europeans invest more in Russia than Russians invest in Europe. This is significant, as EU investments in Russia represent a greater vulnerability to European economic security than do Russian

Figure 3.2
Stock of European FDI and Portfolio Investment in Russia, US$ billions (2013)

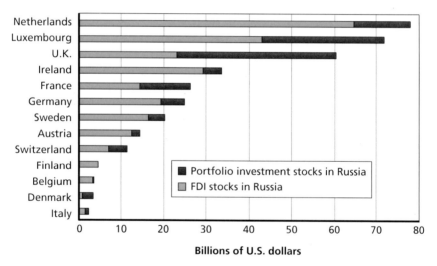

Billions of U.S. dollars

SOURCES: Central Bank of Russia and IMF.
NOTE: This figure excludes Cyprus and countries with FDI and/or portfolio investment stocks in Russia of less than 1 billion U.S. dollars.
RAND RR1305-3.2

---

[14] "Amid Sanctions Battle, Russia Courts Cyprus," STRATFOR, February 27, 2015; Olga Razumovskaya, "Cyprus Signs Deal to Let Russian Navy Ships Stop at its Ports," *Wall Street Journal,* February 25, 2015.

investments in the European Union; in the case of the former, Russia could possibly seize European assets or default on debts to the European Union, while in the case of the latter, Russia's only political leverage would be to sell its own assets in the European Union.

Indeed, this threat is not wholly without merit. In October 2014, a draft law was preliminarily approved in the lower house of the Russian parliament that would permit Moscow to seize foreign assets in the country in retaliation for Western sanctions. The law would allow for these expropriated funds to be used to compensate Russian oligarchs and industrialists whose property or assets abroad had been targeted under the current Western sanctions regime. While the bill still faces many hurdles before becoming law—it must pass the Duma three more times before passing the parliament's upper chamber and being signed by President Putin—the possibility cannot be discounted that this remarkable weapon of retribution could eventually be employed to the detriment of Western companies heavily invested in Russia.[15]

Some EU banks are vulnerable to losses stemming from financial sanctions targeting Russian state-owned banks. Large European banks are expected to lose new business providing financing and other services to Russian banks.[16] These banks might be expected to lobby to reduce financial sanctions on Russia. However, they already have been offloading exposure to Russia.[17] As of the end of October 2014, EU bank exposure to Russia had fallen about 7 percent since the beginning of the year.[18] In absolute terms, the European countries with the largest financial exposure are France (Société Générale), Italy (UniCredit), and Austria (Raiffeisen).[19] However, at least in the short term, European banks with the greatest exposure to Russia have not signaled that they are overly concerned about the impact of sanctions on their profits.

---

[15] Andrew Kramer, "Russia Seeks Sanctions Tit for Tat," *New York Times*, October 8, 2014.

[16] Erik Jones, "EU Sanctions Against Russia Are a Double-Edged Sword," *Moscow Times*, August 3, 2014.

[17] Jones, 2014.

[18] Laurence Norman, "EU Projects Impact of Sanctions on Russian Economy," *Wall Street Journal*, October 29, 2014.

[19] Jones, 2014.

Executives from Raiffeisen Bank International of Austria, Rabobank of the Netherlands, Commerzbank of Germany, Société Générale of France, and Unicredit of Italy have all stated that they expect the impact on earnings to be low or limited; they still view Russia as an attractive banking market in the medium and long term.[20]

Looking at FDI and portfolio investment as percentage of GDP, rather than in value, offers a different perspective (see Figure 3.3). Luxembourg's large financial sector holds Russian FDI and portfolio investment stocks that represent more than 40 percent of its GDP, but this is balanced by its much larger investments in Russia, equivalent to 120 percent of Luxembourg's GDP.

Figure 3.3
FDI and Portfolio Investment Flows between Russia and European Countries, in percentage of their GDP (2013)

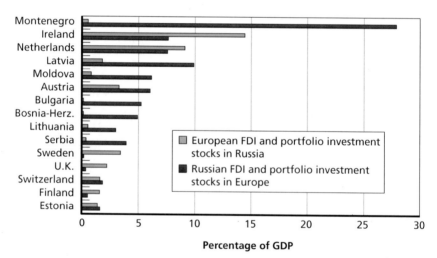

SOURCES: Central Bank of Russia and IMF.
NOTE: This figure excludes Cyprus; Luxembourg; and countries with both FDI and portfolio investment stocks in Russia, or Russian FDI and portfolio investment stocks below 1 percent of their GDP.
RAND RR1305-3.3

---

[20] Chad Bray, "European Banks Expect Only 'Limited' Impact From Sanctions on Russia," *New York Times*, August 21, 2014; Denis Abramov, "How Sanctions Against Russia Have Affected European Companies," *Moscow Times*, August 7, 2014.

Figure 3.3 shows, however, that Russian investments are disproportionately large for a number of small European countries. Russian FDI and portfolio investments in Montenegro are equivalent to 28 percent of the Montenegrin GDP—while Montenegro has very few investments in Russia. In Latvia, they are equivalent to 10 percent of the Latvian GDP, and in Ireland, the Netherlands, Moldova, Austria, Bulgaria, and Bosnia-Herzegovina, they are equivalent to more than 5 percent of GDP. If Russian investors began to move to sell these assets, the localized effect could erode these small economies' support for Western-imposed sanctions.

Conclusion

Except in the case of titanium, EU member states are largely immune to Russian curbs on exports of nonenergy goods, as alternative supplies are available. A small subset of European countries—Lithuania, Finland, Estonia, Poland, and Norway—has been disproportionately affected by Russian countersanctions on agricultural, livestock, and fishery products when compared with other European countries. However, despite these economic costs, these countries have been on the forefront of countries supporting continuing sanctions against Russia, suggesting resilience in the face of economic losses.

European vulnerabilities with regard to financial flows are limited. Cyprus is the most heavily dependent of EU member states on financial flows from Russia, but these flows tend to consist of flows to nonresident accounts owned by Russians and Russian companies. So far Cyprus has not broken EU solidarity on sanctions on Russia. Key banking institutions in Western Europe have signaled that they are not overly concerned about the impact of sanctions on their profits.

CHAPTER FOUR

European Energy Vulnerabilities

End use energy—the forms of energy like motor vehicle fuels and electricity consumed by households and industry—is a crucial input into modern economies.[1] Sharp reductions in the availability of end use energy lead to price spikes that bite into consumer purchasing power or make manufactured products uncompetitive; in the case of refined oil products, they have contributed to recessions. In the worst case, shortages of natural gas and other fuels used for heating can result in homes going cold.

Because of the importance of energy in modern economies, governments are highly concerned about vulnerabilities to reductions in supply. In addition to stockpiling, supporting domestic production, and diversifying sources of supply, governments have incentives to remain on good terms with their major suppliers. Ensuring global supplies of oil from Saudi Arabia and other Persian Gulf suppliers, for instance, has been an important factor in U.S. policy in this part of the world.[2] .In light of the economic importance of energy, the very substantial

---

[1] Refined oil products are primarily used for transportation, while electricity is used for virtually all other purposes. Except in a few marginal applications, the two types of end use energy are not substitutes. Therefore, in our assessments of European reliance on Russian energy, we focus on the share of Russian supplies for specific fuels, such as natural gas, coal, or oil, as that is where European vulnerabilities may lie. We do not calculate the share of EU supplies of total energy provided by Russia, as these aggregate figures do not reflect the economic consequences for a reduction in imports from Russia for EU economies.

[2] Keith Crane, Andreas Goldthau, Michael Toman, Thomas Light, Stuart E. Johnson, Alireza Nader, Angel Rabasa, and Harun Dogo, *Imported Oil and U.S. National Security*, Santa Monica, Calif.: RAND Corporation, MG-838-USCC, 2009.

role that Russian (and Soviet) energy has played in supplying European demand has been a source of concern for EU and NATO member states for decades. During the Soviet era, this concern focused on potential Soviet leverage over European members of NATO, as European desires to ensure steady supplies of oil and natural gas were seen as having the potential to undermine alliance unity. In the 1990s, policy discussions shifted to the reliability of Russia as a supplier because of the deterioration of Russian energy infrastructure and declines in output due to reductions in investment. In the past decade, the focus has been on supply interruptions for natural gas because of disputes between Russia and the transit countries of Belarus and Ukraine. Policymakers are also concerned about the pernicious effects of corruption and graft associated with energy trade in European states.

In this chapter, we evaluate European vulnerabilities stemming from importing energy from Russia. For each imported fuel, the chapter addresses two questions:

1. How important are Russian supplies of the particular type of energy for the economies of EU or NATO member states?
2. To what extent is the European Union—as a whole or particular member states—vulnerable because of the role Russia plays as a source of energy?

Crude Oil and Refined Products

Refined oil products are essential for modern market economies. The transportation sector runs almost exclusively on refined oil products. However, the degree of vulnerability to a cutoff in supplies of crude oil or refined oil products from a particular supplier depends on whether a country can readily find substitute supplies from other sources or has stockpiles on which it can draw to cushion shorter-term disruptions. It also depends on the elasticity of demand: the ease with which consumers can reduce consumption of refined oil products in response to higher prices in the event of a shock to supply.

Europe's Reliance on Russian Crude Oil and Refined Oil Products

The European Union uses imported crude oil to produce refined oil products for export, not just for domestic consumption. It exports about 28 percent of total production on a net basis. It produces only 11 percent of the crude oil that it refines, importing the rest. Russia is the European Union's largest source of oil and refined oil products. In 2013, on a net basis it supplied 35 percent of the crude and refined oil products consumed or exported by the European Union and almost half of net imports.[3]

How Vulnerable is the EU to a Russian Cutoff in Supplies of Oil Refined Oil Products?

Russia could threaten to cut off exports of all oil and refined oil products to the European Union. It could also halt exports through specific pipelines targeting countries served by those pipelines. If Russia could successfully deny these products to the European Union, the economic consequences for the European Union would be severe.

However, in contrast to natural gas, which can be transported only by pipeline or expensive ships or tank cars designed specifically for liquefied natural gas (LNG), crude oil and refined oil products are fairly easy to transport. The European Union as a whole has a large, modern system of terminals, refineries, and pipelines that handle enormous quantities of crude oil and refined oil products. The larger EU refineries tend to be equipped with specialized units to "crack" heavier crudes or remove sulfur from sour crudes, allowing them to adjust their operations to accept crudes somewhat different from their normal supplies. As crude oil and refined oil products are globally traded commodities, EU refineries are able to draw on a wide range of imported crudes to maintain their operations.

Because of this existing infrastructure, Western Europe's oil industry has great flexibility in terms of processing alternative sources of crude supply and handling disruptions to customary patterns of supply. Thus, EU member states would not face substantial costs if Russia embargoed oil sales to EU or NATO member states. Global

---

[3]   RAND calculations based on data from Eurostat.

oil markets are integrated: Diverting current sales by Russia to other markets would free up oil formerly sold in those markets for sale to EU member states.

To counter the ability of EU member states to substitute oil from other sources in response to a cutoff, Russia could choose to halt all its exports of oil and refined oil products. As the second-largest exporter of oil and refined oil products in the world, Russia's cutoff of exports would result in a shock to global supply that would lead to a surge in world market prices of oil, slowing growth or precipitating a global recession. But such a move would have even more catastrophic consequences for the Russian economy. Producing and refining oil accounts for as much as a fifth of Russia's GDP; oil and refined oil products comprise half of Russia's exports, so a decision on the part of the Russian government to cease exporting all oil and refined oil products seems highly unlikely.

Alternatively, Russia could stop shipping oil to Central Europe through specific pipelines so as to target particular states. The *Druzhba* (or Friendship) pipeline, or really pipelines, bifurcates within Russia, with one branch traversing Belarus to Poland, ending in eastern Germany, and the other crossing Ukraine, where it bifurcates again to Slovakia and Hungary. All the major refineries in the former Warsaw Pact states are served by the *Druzhba*.[4] If this pipeline were to be closed, these refineries would have to transport alternative sources of crude oil at greater cost to make up for the absence of Russian crude. These Central European refineries have alternative pipeline connections to ports, but the capacity of these alternative pipelines would be insufficient to permit them to operate at capacity, imposing financial costs on these companies.

However, the European Union would be able to respond to such a move thanks to the considerable excess refining capacity of its member states. If Russia were to stop exporting oil to Central European EU member states, current EU refined oil output would be more than enough to cover EU demand, leaving a much smaller, but still sub-

---

[4]   European Chemical Site Promotion Platform, *An Overview of the Pipeline Networks of Europe*, undated.

stantial, export surplus. Refining output could also be increased by operating these refineries at closer-to-capacity levels. This would not be easy: The EU refining industry would have to readjust existing production and distribution patterns, increasing output of refined products from coastal refineries with ready access to seaborne crude oil and moving these refined products into Central Europe to compensate for reduced output from refineries situated on the *Druzhba* pipeline. However, Russia would be in even more difficult straits, as its existing port capacity and pipelines to ports are too small to handle all the oil currently exported by pipeline. Consequently, a Russian decision to stop shipping oil to Central European states would impose more substantial costs on Russia (in terms of lower exports) than on its intended targets.

Natural Gas

Europe's Reliance on Russian Gas

On a net basis, the European Union imported two-thirds of the natural gas it consumed in 2013. Of this amount, 41 percent came from Russia. EU imports of Russian natural gas were equivalent to about 27 percent of total EU consumption in 2013.[5] However, imports of natural gas from Russia were higher than average in 2013; over the course of the past decade, Russia supplied 20 percent to 25 percent of EU gas consumption.

In terms of volumes and their value to Gazprom, Germany, Italy, and Turkey are the largest European importers of Russian natural gas (Figure 4.1). Distantly following are the economies of Poland, France, the Czech Republic, Hungary, Austria, the Slovak Republic, the Netherlands, and Finland.

On a percentage basis, the share of Russian imports in total consumption of natural gas of the smaller economies of southeastern, Central, and Northern Europe is generally higher, sometimes substantially so, than those of Western Europe. Western Europe produces a substantial share of the natural gas it consumes domestically. The Netherlands,

---

[5]   RAND calculations based on data from Eurostat.

Figure 4.1
European Natural Gas Imports, by Source, in 2013 (billion cubic meters)

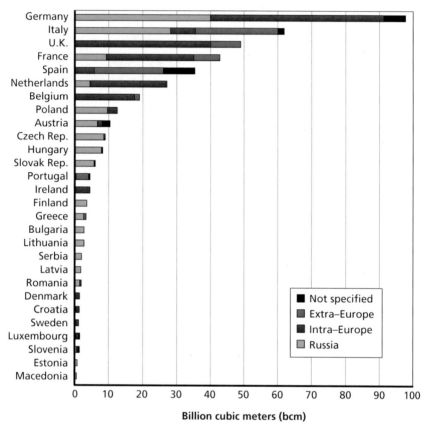

SOURCE: Eurostat, undated.
RAND RR1305-4.1

the United Kingdom, Germany, Italy, and Denmark all produce some natural gas. Norway is a major source of imports for Western Europe. Western Europe also pipes in natural gas from Algeria and Libya and receives supplies of LNG from Nigeria, Qatar, Egypt, and Trinidad and Tobago, as well as Algeria and Libya.

The countries that rely most heavily on Russia and have limited or no access to alternative supplies are the Baltic states and southeastern Europe (see Figure 4.2). Natural gas plays a relatively small role in over-

Figure 4.2
Russian Supplies, as a Percentage of Total Gas Imports in Europe

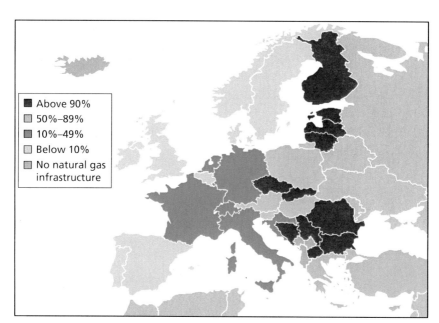

SOURCES: Eurostat, undated; International Energy Agency, undated; Gazprom Export, undated; RAND calculations.
RAND RR1305-4.2

all energy supplies in some of the countries that rely heavily on Russian gas. However, imported gas may still play a critical role for particular purposes, such as district heating.[6]

How Vulnerable is Europe to the Consequences of a Russian Gas Cutoff?

Given the importance of Russian gas supplies for many European states, how harmful would a disruption of these imports be to their economies? That is, how vulnerable are European states—individually and collectively—to a potential total Russian cutoff or reduction in the supply of natural gas or through specific pipelines?

---

[6]   International Monetary Fund, "Russian Federation: Staff Report for the 2014 Article IV Consultation," IMF Country Report No. 14/175, Washington, D.C., June 11, 2014, p. 19.

The extent to which the European Union is vulnerable to a cutoff in Russian supplies of natural gas depends on

1. the availability of other sources of natural gas
2. the possibility of substituting other forms of energy for supplies of natural gas that have been curtailed
3. the severity of the consequences for the economy if no substitutes for the missing natural gas can be found.

The harder it is to find alternative supplies of natural gas, the fewer alternative fuels that can be used to replace natural gas. Therefore, the more critical the fuel for businesses and households, the more vulnerable EU member states are to a cutoff.

One in-depth analysis of the potential for Europe to do without natural gas imported from Russia is the Oxford Institute of Energy Studies (OIES)'s "Reducing European Dependence on Russian Gas: Distinguishing Natural Gas Security from Geopolitics."[7] The focus of the study is whether Europe could cost-effectively stop importing natural gas from Russia. Comparative costs play an important role in the analysis. The study concludes that imports from Russia will remain a highly competitive source of natural gas for EU member states and that displacing imports of natural gas from Russia would be difficult and expensive.

A study by the European Commission in July 2014 analyzed how EU member states would fare in the event of a six-month cutoff in natural gas imports from Russia followed by a two-week cold snap. The study investigated two scenarios, one in which each country goes it alone and a second in which member states cooperate by sharing gas supplies.[8] The study concludes that if member states were to go it alone,

---

[7] Ralf Dickel, Elham Hassanzadeh, James Henderson, Anouk Honoré, Laura El-Katiri, Simon Pirani, Howard Rogers, Jonathan Stern, and Katja Yafimava, "Reducing European Dependence on Russian Gas: Distinguishing Natural Gas Security from Geopolitics," OIES Paper: NG 92, Oxford, UK: Oxford Institute for Energy Studies, University of Oxford, October 2014, p. 1.

[8] European Commission, "Communication from the Commission to the European Parliament and the Council on the Short Term Resilience of the European Gas System Pre-

the Baltic states and several states in southeastern Europe would face severe problems with providing citizens and businesses with sufficient natural gas. If member states were to cooperate, the most severe impact of the cutoff and cold snap would be mitigated.

We conduct our own analysis of EU vulnerabilities to a cutoff in imports of Russian natural gas, addressing different questions than those posed by the OIES and European Commission studies. Whereas the OIES report assesses the cost and feasibility of an EU decision to forgo the import of Russian gas, we evaluate the economic consequences for EU member states of a Russian decision to cut off imports. Whereas the European Commission study assesses the consequences of a six-month interruption in Russian supplies of gas, we evaluate the consequences for EU member states of a cutoff of indeterminate length.

We draw on Eurostat and other data on patterns of natural gas and energy consumption by country, substitutability of alternative fuels, pipelines, and alternative sources of supply for our analysis. We also draw on data from the OIES and European Commission studies. We posit that the European Union would have to replace 110 bcm of natural gas annually, if Russia were to cut off natural gas exports to the European Union. This is the average amount of natural gas imported from Russia between 2009 and 2012. We argue that the 126 bcm imported in 2013 was an anomaly due to a colder winter.[9] To cope with a cutoff of Russian gas of this magnitude for an extended period of time, EU member states would have to find alternative supplies, substitute other fuels, or economize on the use of natural gas. We explore each of these options below.

Supply-Side Responses

The International Energy Agency, the U.S. Energy Information Administration, and both studies outlined above find that the prospects for increasing domestic production of conventional natural gas or increasing imports from Norway, Algeria, or Libya, the non-Russian export-

---

paredness for a Possible Disruption of Supplies from the East During the Fall and Winter of 2014/2015," SWD(2014) 322 Final, Brussels, October 16, 2014.

[9]   RAND calculations based on data from Eurostat.

ers currently connected to the European Union by pipeline, are very limited. However, other solutions exist. By 2019 the Trans-Anatolian Natural Gas Pipeline—begun in 2015—should be completed. When finished, it will move 16 bcm of gas from Azerbaijan to Turkey (6 bcm) and then on to Europe (10 bcm).[10] The European Union could also theoretically cover the entire shortfall associated with a cutoff in Russian exports of natural gas by importing more LNG. The European Union has more than 200 bcm in capacity for regasifying LNG, and more is being constructed; global trade in LNG ran 299 bcm in 2013, out of which the European Union accounted for 43 bcm, 14 percent, leaving 256 bcm in potential additional supplies.[11] However, covering the entire shortfall with imports of LNG would be an expensive solution. The spot market for LNG is much smaller and less liquid than that for oil. Consequently, increased demand for LNG would push up prices. The International Energy Agency estimates that purchasing LNG on spot markets to cover 40 percent of a shortfall in the European Union could result in doubling prevailing spot market prices.[12] The Commission report argues that because of these price pressures, imports of LNG could be doubled, but not more.[13] Consequently, we assume that the European Union could obtain an additional 43 bcm, equivalent to 17 percent of current non-EU global consumption of LNG, to help cover a shortfall stemming from a halt to Russian exports of natural gas to the European Union.

Substituting Alternative Fuels for Natural Gas

Unlike refined oil products, which are predominantly consumed by the transportation sector, natural gas is consumed by a variety of end users. In 2012, about 30 percent of natural gas in the European Union was consumed by district heating companies and residential users, pri-

---

[10] Isabel Gorst, "Construction of Tanap Pipeline Begins in Turkey as EU and Russia Spar for Upper Hand," *Financial Times*, March 18, 2015.

[11] International Group of Liquefied Natural Gas Importers, *The LNG Industry, 2013*, Neuilly-sur-Seine, France: GIIGNL, 2013, p. 13.

[12] European Commission, 2014, p. 12.

[13] European Commission, 2014, p. 12.

marily for space and water heating; 11 percent by commercials users, mainly for the same ends; 28 percent by industry, primarily for process heat and in the chemical industry; 30 percent for electric power generation; and 1 percent for "other," primarily transportation (Figure 4.3).

Of these uses, it would be almost impossible to substitute alternative fuels for natural gas in the commercial, residential, and transportation sectors: 88 percent of natural gas used by residential and commercial consumers is combusted in individual furnaces, hot water heaters, and boilers that run only on natural gas. Not surprisingly, residential use is considered "protected" by EU governments: Residential users are given first priority in the event of any shortfall in supplies of natural gas. For the European Union as a whole, domestic production and non-Russian imports are more than adequate to cover demand for natural gas for heating and hot water. However, as will be discussed

Figure 4.3
European Consumption of Natural Gas by Sector (2012)

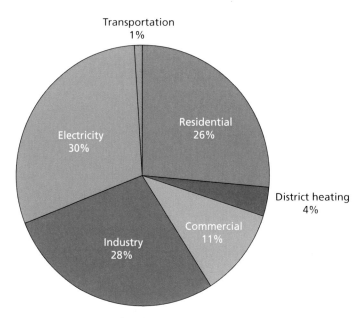

SOURCE: Eurostat, undated.
RAND RR1503-4.3

later in this chapter, some individual countries that depend heavily on Russian imports could have difficulties providing heat and hot water. In most cases, the district heating or combined heat and power plants that combust the remaining 12 percent of gas consumed for purposes of heating and providing hot water are able to substitute fuel oil (diesel) for natural gas. For example, Finland has deliberately designed its district heating plants for both fuels. Fuel switching in these plants could reduce overall natural gas demand by 3.6 percent, equivalent to about 17 bcm or 15 percent of imports from Russia.

Based on consumption by industry in 2004 of fuel oil, which has since been replaced by natural gas, the OIES study places a theoretical upper bound of 27 bcm of industrial and commercial consumption of natural gas that might be replaced by fuel oil in the case of a cutoff.[14] However, because of retirements of equipment that can use both fuels, the actual scope for substitution of fuel oil for natural gas is probably considerably less.

The European electric power sector consumed 142 bcm in 2012, 30 percent of all the natural gas consumed in the European Union. In contrast to most of the other sectors, there are a number of alternative sources that could be substituted for natural gas in this sector: coal, nuclear, biomass, hydropower, solar, and wind. Because demand for electricity has fallen in the European Union over the last several years, down 3.4 percent from 2008 through 2013, excess generating capacity exists for these other fuel types, especially coal. In addition, despite the declines in power consumption, many EU member states have invested heavily in renewable energy capacity over the past several years.[15] Renewable energy rose 73 percent from 2004 through 2013 and 39 percent from 2008 through 2013. By 2013, it generated 83 percent as much electricity as natural gas. Substituting coal or renewables to generate electricity could compensate for some of the natural gas used in power generation. However, there has already been substantial substitution: The share of electricity generated from gas has fallen from 24 percent in 2008 to about 15 percent in 2013. Despite this

---

[14] Dickel et al., 2014, p. 42.

[15] RAND calculations based on data from Eurostat.

caveat, the OIES study states that in a highly favorable environment, the European Union could *theoretically* replace as much as 50 bcm to 60 bcm of natural gas currently used to generate electricity.[16]

Reductions in Demand

Natural gas is important for peaking capacity. Measures to smooth demand would permit other sources of primary energy in electricity generation to more easily substitute for natural gas. Improvements in grid management and changes in operating procedures for coal-fired power plants over the past decade have made it easier to use demand management as a replacement for the use of natural gas for peaking capacity.

If industrial users are unable to use fuel oil because of divestment of dual-use equipment or because of cost *in extremis*, companies could close down operations to save natural gas. In this case, the 27 bcm saved by substituting fuel oil for natural gas in industrial applications would be saved by shutting down industrial operations.

Aggregate EU Bottom Line

Table 4.1 compares all these alternative measures to make up for a potential shortfall in Russian gas with Russian import volumes.

Looking at the European Union as a whole, it appears that by employing a range of measures, the European Union could compensate for a complete cutoff in imports of natural gas from Russia. The most important measures would be increasing imports of LNG and reducing the consumption of natural gas in generating electricity. In addition, substituting fuel oil for natural gas in industrial applications or, if need be, shutting down industries that rely on natural gas, would make a substantial contribution to bridging the supply gap. However, with the exception of deliveries in 2019 and beyond through the Trans-Anatolian Natural Gas Pipeline, all of these measures would be substantially more expensive, possibly twice as expensive or more, than imported natural gas from Russia.

---

[16] Dickel et al., 2014, p. 45.

Table 4.1
How the European Union Could Cope with a Cutoff in Russian
Exports of Natural Gas

Source	Amount (BCM)
Trans-Anatolian Natural Gas Pipeline (starting in 2019)	10
Increased imports of LNG	43
Substituting fuel oil in district heating plants	17
Substituting fuel oil for industrial and commercial uses	27
Substituting other sources of electricity	50
Theoretical maximum	147
Russian imports	110
Difference	37

SOURCE: RAND calculations.

Individual Countries

Although in aggregate, the European Union could weather a cutoff in Russian exports of natural gas, albeit at some cost, those countries that rely completely or mainly on imports of Russian natural gas could face serious economic and social challenges. Figure 4.4 shows projected shortfalls of natural gas facing the most vulnerable or affected EU member states (Bulgaria, Estonia, Finland, Greece, Hungary, Latvia, Lithuania, Macedonia, Poland, and Romania) for the two scenarios developed in the European Commission report.

Using more detailed information, we assess the overall dependence on natural gas in the overall nonoil energy mix of these countries (except for Bosnia-Herzegovina, for which we lack information) according to protected and unprotected uses. For the purposes of this analysis, we define *protected* uses as all gas consumed in combined heat and power plants, under the assumption that the heat needs to be generated for residential heating, district heating plants, and commercial and residential users.[17] Such users are considered the highest priority by

---

[17] The European Commission study on the short-term resilience of the European gas system notes that "The Security of Gas Supply Regulation established a category of so-called pro-

Figure 4.4
Projected Shortfalls of Natural Gas in the Event of a Cutoff of Russian Supplies

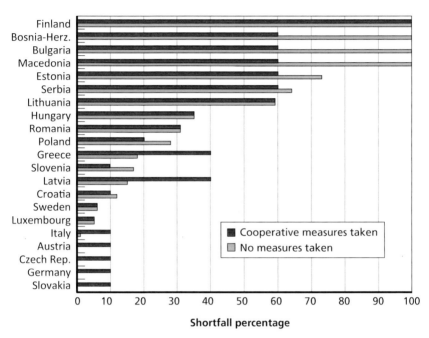

Shortfall percentage

SOURCE: European Commission, 2014; RAND calculations.
RAND RR1305-4.4

their respective governments. *Unprotected* uses include natural gas used in industry or to generate electricity.

As can be seen in Figure 4.5, the role of natural gas in overall nonoil industry looms largest in Lithuania, Hungary, Romania, and Latvia. More than half of all nonoil energy in Lithuania is provided by natural gas. However, most natural gas in Lithuania is not used by protected users, but by industry and the electric power sector; only 17 percent of natural gas is used by combined heat and power plants, district

tected customers which includes households and, when the Member States so decide, essential social services and SMEs, within a certain limit, and district heating installations that cannot switch fuels and that deliver heat to other protected customers." See European Commission, 2014, footnote. 21, p. 9.

Figure 4.5
The Role of Natural Gas in Nonoil Energy Balances in Vulnerable Countries

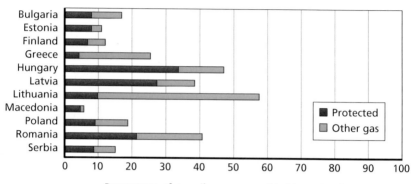

Percentage of nonoil energy provided by natural gas

SOURCE: Eurostat, undated.
RAND RR1305-4.5

heating, or residential and commercial users. Close to half of all nonoil energy consumed in Hungary is provided by natural gas. In contrast to Lithuania, 71 percent of this natural gas goes to protected users, making Hungary particularly vulnerable to a cutoff in natural gas supplies. Hungary produces some natural gas domestically, but all of its imports come from Russia. Romania and Latvia depend less on natural gas than Lithuania and Hungary; natural gas accounts for about 40 percent of total nonoil energy consumption in both countries. In both cases, most natural gas is consumed by protected users.

Natural gas plays a much smaller role in the overall nonoil energy balance in the other countries, ranging from 5.6 percent in the case of Macedonia to 25.4 percent in Greece. In the cases of Bulgaria, Greece, and Poland, protected uses account for less than half of total consumption of natural gas. However, in the case of the remaining countries (Estonia, Finland, Macedonia, and Serbia), protected uses account for the greatest share of consumption.

Figure 4.6 shows the degree of self-sufficiency of these countries. As can be seen, only Romania produces more natural gas than is consumed by protected users. In all other countries, protected uses greatly exceed domestic production. This gas is imported, almost exclusively

Figure 4.6
Shares of Protected Uses and Domestic Production in Natural Gas Consumption in Vulnerable Countries

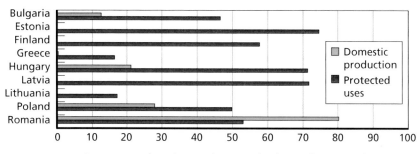

Percentage of total natural gas production and consumption

SOURCE: Eurostat, undated.
NOTE: Although we capture all use of natural gas in Figure 3.5, we show these uses as shares of total energy consumption minus consumption of oil and refined oil products, which we assumed are used almost exclusively for transportation.
RAND RR1305-4.6

from or through Russia. Only Greece and, to a lesser extent, Poland import appreciable amounts of gas from non-Russian sources. The chart also shows the importance of protected uses in overall consumption of natural gas: In all these countries except Greece and Lithuania, protected uses account for half or more of overall consumption of natural gas. In short, Estonia, Finland, Hungary, Latvia, Lithuania, and Poland are the EU member states most vulnerable to a cutoff of natural gas from Russia.

Yet, a number of options exist in the medium-to-long term for these countries to limit their vulnerability to a Russian gas cutoff. The OIES study notes that LNG terminals to be built in Lithuania and Poland over the 2015–2030 time frame will make it possible to import LNG to the Baltic region, hence reducing its reliance on Russian gas— albeit at a higher cost.[18] The European Commission study also shows that EU cooperative measures can significantly reduce the impact of a short-term cutoff on those EU member states most affected.[19]

---

[18] Dickel et al., 2014, p. 40.

[19] European Commission, 2014, p. 6.

Other Energy Sources and Products

Compared to crude oil and natural gas, the European Union is relatively self-sufficient in coal. In 2013, 73 percent of the coal consumed in the European Union was mined domestically. Russia has become one of the most important suppliers of imported coal. In 2013, the European Union imported 68.3 million metric tons of coal from Russia, 33 percent of net imports and 9 percent of EU consumption.[20]

Most countries in the world mine some coal; dozens are exporters. The major exporters (Australia, Indonesia, Colombia, South Africa, and the United States) have the ability to ramp up production, especially at the current moment when demand in the two largest markets, China and the United States, has fallen. Like oil, coal is easily transported by rail or ship. Consequently, if Russia were to halt exports of coal to EU member states, they could easily obtain and transport supplies from alternative suppliers.

In recent years, Russia has provided from 2 percent to 4 percent of total EU imports of electricity, less than 1 percent of total EU consumption. Russian exports of electricity have gone disproportionately to four countries: Finland, Latvia, Lithuania, and Estonia[21]—the only EU member states directly linked to the Russian grid—and a very small amount to part of Norway. The Baltic countries remain part of the grid that covers Belarus, Kaliningrad, and northwestern Russia in addition to themselves (the BRELL circuit). In 2012, Lithuania received 23 percent of its power from Russia, and Latvia 17 percent; Estonia did not import electricity from Russia directly but benefited from re-exports from its neighbors.[22] The countries do import power from the European Union through transmission lines connecting them to Poland and Sweden. In addition, Finland imports 5 percent of its power from

---

[20] RAND calculations from Eurostat.

[21] Estonia is not connected to Russia directly by a transmission line but receives electricity generated in Russia through its connection with the other Baltic states.

[22] Eurostat, undated.

Russia, but it is also connected to the Inter-Nordic power system that connects it to Sweden, Norway, and Eastern Denmark.[23]

As with natural gas, existing connections determine whether or not a state is able to obtain alternative supplies in the event of a cutoff. These four countries are also linked to the EU grid, so some redundancy exists in the system. The Baltic states would face strains on their electricity systems if Russia were to sever grid connections. However, Russia could do so only by also cutting off Kaliningrad. It would also have to invest in linking northwestern Russia and Belarus to other parts of the Russian grid.

Western Energy Companies and Russia

In addition to the potential coercive leverage that Russia may have on EU member states due to its large role as an energy supplier, Russia has the potential to exercise leverage over EU members through the inducements it can provide to EU energy companies. Opening opportunities for investments in Russia provides incentives to Western oil and gas companies to lobby their home governments to take policy stances more favorable to Russia. As large energy companies play important roles in the economies of several large European countries, these companies have political influence.[24] The United Kingdom's British Petroleum, the Netherlands' Royal Dutch Shell, France's Total, Norway's Statoil, Italy's ENI, Spain's Repsol, and Germany's E.On, RWE, and BASF's Wintershal subsidiary are among the largest companies in their respective countries. Because of Russia's massive oil and gas reserves, Russian energy companies have been attractive partners for these companies.

Western sanctions on Russia are likely to impose costs on major Western oil companies as well as on Russia. Overall, however, sanctions in the energy sector have not yet had a significant effect on these companies' business dealings with Russia. First, the sanctions do not

---

[23] Fingrid, "Power System in Finland," website, undated.

[24] On this issue, see, for instance, Rawi Abdelal, "The Profits of Power: Commerce and Realpolitik in Eurasia," *Review of International Political Economy*, Vol. 20, No. 3, 2013.

apply to agreements signed between European and Russian firms before August 1, 2014. Second, sanctions in the energy sector are limited to the transfer of oil exploration technologies. They have been designed to impede Russia's ability to pursue long-term exploration projects through two mechanisms: (1) embargoing the transfers of selected Western technologies and equipment required for deep-sea oil drilling, oil shale extraction, and Arctic Shelf exploration; and (2) increasing the cost of financing for Russian energy firms, which have increasingly become reliant on "prefinancing deals," by which loans are repaid with revenues from future oil supplies after the completion of new projects. This being said, Western European energy executives have warned that current conditions could change and that future investments could be harmed by the imposition of additional sanctions.[25]

Some countries are facing higher costs from the sanctions than others. Norway's Statoil has a number of joint projects with Russia in the Arctic. An agreement signed in 2010 between the two countries and settling a 40-year-long territorial dispute gave Norway an additional 54,000 square miles of continental shelf to explore. However, it binds the two countries into working jointly to exploit cross-border oil and gas deposits.[26] Norway has also provided advanced technology to help Russia develop offshore oil deposits. Yet, Norway—not an EU member—has enforced the same sanctions as the European Union.[27] Norway's recent discovery of potentially large reserves in its north, as well as the low prices of oil (which make it less urgent to focus on the technically difficult and expensive exploration and extraction of

---

[25] "Thriving BP Worried by Impact of Harsher Sanctions on Rosneft Ties," *Moscow Times*, July 29, 2014.

[26] Walter Gibbs, "Russia and Norway Reach Accord on Barents Sea," *New York Times*, April 27, 2010; Energy Information Administration, "Norway," web page, U.S. Department of Energy, April 28, 2014.

[27] Norwegian Ministry of Foreign Affairs, "Norway Tightens Restrictive Measures Against Russia," press release, October 10, 2014.

resources in the Arctic), may lessen the impact of the sanctions against Russia on its domestic oil industry.[28]

The European Union's strained relations with Russia have created difficulties for Hungary as well. Hungary successfully negotiated a new gas supply agreement with Russia in 2015 when Putin visited Budapest. In January 2004, Hungary entered into discussions concerning an agreement with two Russian companies with close ties to Putin to expand the country's nuclear power plant at Paks, as well as to provide the expanded facility with enriched nuclear fuel.[29] However, as the Ukrainian crisis intensified, Hungary has come under increasing pressure to curtail economic cooperation with Russia and adopt a tougher line toward Moscow. In March, the European Union blocked the 12 billion–euro nuclear power plants deal, throwing a spanner in the works of a project that Hungarian Prime Minister Viktor Orbán had put at the center of his strategy to build closer ties to Russia. The decision exacerbated tensions between Hungary and the European Commission. To revive the plan Hungary would need to negotiate a new fuel contract or pursue legal action against the commission.[30]

Conclusion

Russia is the largest supplier of both oil and natural gas to EU member states. Despite the large role played by Russia in supplying EU member states with oil and refined oil products, in the event of a complete cutoff of Russian supplies, European member states would be able to find alternative sources of supply at market prices. Central European refineries linked to Russia by pipeline would face supply disruptions mitigated by increased output from coastal refineries elsewhere in Europe.

---

[28] Richard Milne, "Lundin Makes 'Game-Changer' Oil Discovery in Norwegian Arctic," *Financial Times*, October 14, 2014; James F. Collins, Ross A. Virginia, and Kenneth Yalowitz, "Hands Across the Melting Ice," *New York Times*, May 13, 2013.

[29] Anthony Faiola, "From Russia with Love: An Energy Deal for Hungary," *Washington Post*, February 16, 2015.

[30] Andrew Byrne and Christian Oliver, "Brussels Veto of Hungarian Nuclear Deal to Inflame Tensions with Russia," *Financial Times*, March 13, 2015.

Moreover, because of the large role played by the oil industry in the Russian economy, a Russian embargo on exports of oil and refined oil products would be very expensive. In the case of natural gas, pipelines physically tie European customers to Russia. The European Commission has made investments in connecting pipelines and has encouraged member states to develop alternative sources of supply, especially LNG terminals, and take other steps to mitigate the consequences of a disruption in natural gas supplied by Russia. With some difficulty, EU European states could cope with a complete, long-term cutoff in Russian supplies of natural gas. However, several states in southeastern or Central Europe would face sizable adjustment costs. The electric power grid of the Baltic republics is part of a grid connecting them with Belarus, Kaliningrad, and northwestern Russia. Conceivably, Russia could cut this connection but would have to first invest in integrating electric power distribution on its own territory to grids in other regions of Russia. Finally, Russia could potentially leverage offers of access to its large reserves of oil and natural gas to induce European energy companies to lobby their governments to adopt policies more favorable to Russia—but as of 2015, such lobbying appeared still a long way from jeopardizing EU member states' unity on the sanctions policy toward Russia.

CHAPTER FIVE

Political Vulnerabilities

European countries have different levels of vulnerability and offer various entry points for Russian overt and covert influence. One is the presence of disaffected national minorities susceptible to Russian manipulation. Another is the rise of extremist political parties on the right and left that have adopted pro-Russian stances in local, national, and European elections. This chapter examines the dangers and significance for Russian manipulation of these vulnerabilities.

Minority Issues

As noted earlier, the large ethnic Russian and Russophone minorities in Estonia and Latvia provide a lever that Russia could use to attempt to exert pressure on these two Baltic states.[1] When the Baltic states regained their independence, the new Estonian and Latvian governments saw the Russophones as a foreign element, a legacy and a tool of the Soviet occupation, and a potential mechanism for subverting the independence of these states. The new governments did not automatically give these people citizenship—and thus a right to vote and a role in shaping directly the political course of their countries. Only in Lithuania, where there were far fewer Russophones, and thus a much lower potential threat to the new state from the Soviet-era migrants, did the

---

[1] Estonia and Latvia experienced an influx of migrants—Russians, Belarusians, Ukrainians, and Tatars, all using Russian as the lingua franca—during their time as Soviet republics (1945–1991).

new government give all Soviet-era inhabitants Lithuanian citizenship. Putin has stressed Moscow's responsibility to protect the welfare of ethnic Russians and Russian speakers living outside Russia's borders. Estonian and Latvian officials fear that Russia could use the alleged mistreatment of the Russian minority as a pretext for making political demands on the two countries.

As discussed earlier in Chapter Two, it is possible that Russia could attempt to foment insurgency in Estonia and Latvia by leveraging the discontent that already exists among Russophone minorities in these two countries—even though many, perhaps most, of the Russians in these areas have no interest in joining Russia. Russia could instigate protests against the Estonian and Latvian governments and raise the specter of secession in order to increase the pressure on these governments to adopt more accommodating policies that reflect Russian interests. There is also a danger that Russia could infiltrate some of the political parties to reach that same objective.

In Estonia and Latvia, there are large Russian-dominated political parties. In Estonia, Russians have increasingly dominated the Centre Party led by Edgar Savisaar, though Estonia historically has a history of political cleavages crossing ethnic lines. In Latvia, Harmony Centre was the single largest party in the last elections and controls the municipal government of the capital, Riga. The mainstream Latvian parties consistently have excluded the Harmony Centre party from governing coalitions, leading to the ethnic divide as the main political cleavage in Latvia. Harmony Centre and the Centre Party have ties with Putin's United Russia party, and there are frequently voiced, but unsubstantiated, fears that allowing these parties into the coalition would pose a security risk.[2]

Finally, the Russian minorities issue in Latvia and Estonia may also threaten EU unity. Many western EU states either do not agree fully with the way that Latvia and Estonia have gone about treating the Russophone minorities in those countries, or they want them to be more "pragmatic" in their policies. Russia can use subtle propa-

---

[2] "How to Deal with Harmony," *Economist*, October 6, 2014; Richard Milne, "Party with Ties to Putin Pushes Ahead in Estonian Polls," *Financial Times,* February 27, 2015.

ganda and existing political mechanisms to create a situation for the Latvian and Estonian governments whereby they will face pressure from major EU countries (for example, Germany, as it is highly sensitive to any signs of "provocation" of the Russians) to give in and "compromise." Behind the scenes, the major EU countries, such as Germany, could voice their disapproval of Latvian and Estonian minority policies, should the situation of the Russophone minority deteriorate into a more openly conflictive relationship. For reasons of appealing to their domestic constituencies, the coalition governments in Estonia and Latvia will find it very difficult to "compromise" on this issue, as they see it as a question of basic national sovereignty and national survival—hence creating tensions within the Alliance, and possibly far-reaching doubts in major EU/NATO countries about the wisdom of supporting the main policy lines of these countries toward their Russian minorities.

Russia may also be tempted to instrumentalize minority issues in Central Europe. Hungarian Prime Minister Viktor Orbán has moved in an increasingly authoritarian and nationalist direction since 2010,[3] raising concerns that his nationalist rhetoric might inflame the Hungarian minority issue. Hungarian minorities, a legacy of the Trianon Treaty (1920) that followed Hungary's defeat in World War I, are mainly present in Slovakia, Romania, Serbia, and Ukraine. EU officials were particularly dismayed by a speech Orbán made in May 2014 in which he called on Ukraine "to give its minorities, including Hungarians, their due. That is, dual citizenship, collective rights, and autonomy."[4] The statement was widely interpreted, especially in Ukraine, as supporting Russian calls for far-reaching "autonomy" for eastern Ukraine. The danger is that this emotionally charged hot-button political issue could be exploited by right-wing extremists to bolster their internal support and could have a destabilizing spillover effect on Slovakia, Romania, and Ukraine.

---

[3] For a detailed discussion, see Abby Innes, "Hungary's Illiberal Democracy," *Current History*, Vol. 114, No. 770, March 2015, pp. 95–100.

[4] "Orban Renews Autonomy Call for Ethnic Hungarians in Ukraine," Reuters, May 17, 2014.

Russian Links with European Populist and Extremist Parties

An additional potential source of Russian leverage on the domestic politics of European countries is through the populist and extremist parties that have significantly increased their strength in Europe over the past decade. The rise of Marine Le Pen's National Front in France has been the most dramatic example of this trend. But populist parties have also done well in Denmark, Austria, the Netherlands, Hungary, Switzerland, Serbia, the Czech Republic, and Finland.

A number of these parties have expressed their support for Putin's annexation of Crimea. The National Front, for instance, described it as legitimate based on the history of the region.[5] A pro-Moscow nongovernmental organization (NGO) based in Belgium invited the National Front and other far-right parties—including the Freedom Party of Austria (Freiheitliche Partei Österreichs, FPÖ), Vlaams Belang from Belgium, and Jobbik from Hungary—to monitor the March 16, 2014 referendum in Crimea. The team of observers announced that the referendum had been free and fair.[6]

Pro-Russian sentiments in such parties predate the Ukraine crisis. The National Front has long proposed a close strategic partnership with Russia, based on its vision of a "European civilization" whose borders differ from the European Union's and stretch instead from Brest in France to Vladivostok in Russia.[7] During her visit to Moscow in June 2013, Marine Le Pen was received by Duma President Sergei Naryshkin and Chairman of the International Affairs Committee of the Duma Alexei Pushkov.[8] Their exchanges highlighted common views on for-

---

[5] Julien Licourt, "L'Indéfectible Soutien du FN à la Russie de Poutine," *Le Figaro*, March 19, 2014; Benjamin Fox, "Russia Invites EU Far-Right To Observe Crimea Vote," *EU Observer*, March 13, 2014.

[6] Mitchell A. Orenstein, "Putin's Western Allies," *Foreign Affairs*, March 25, 2014; Fox, 2014; Andrew Higgins, "Far-Right Fever for a Europe Tied to Russia," *New York Times*, May 20, 2014.

[7] Licourt, 2014.

[8] Emmanuel Grynszpan, "Moscou déroule le tapis rouge devant Marine Le Pen," *Le Figaro*, June 20, 2013. According to National Front Foreign Affairs Spokesman Ludovic de Danne,

eign policy—a nonintervention policy in Syria, for example—as well as domestic issues, such as the opposition to same-sex marriage.[9] The relation between the National Front and Russia intensified after the Ukrainian crisis, with Marine Le Pen taking two more trips to Moscow in 2014. In December 2014, the National Front admitted to receiving an $11.7 million loan from a Russian bank.[10]

Moscow has offered a sign to far-right parties that their support is most welcome. In December 2013, a representative from Putin's party, United Russia, attended the congress of Italy's Lega Nord, along with several leaders of European far-right parties (including Geert Wilders of the Dutch Partij voor di Vrijheid [Party for Freedom] [PVV] and FPÖ's Heinz-Christian Strache).[11] In April 2014, Putin expressed his satisfaction at the good results obtained by the National Front at the French municipal elections.[12] Putin's interest in Europe's far-right parties may have several motives, including increasing Russian influence on Western European politics, weakening NATO, promoting anti-American views, showing Russia's domestic audience that its leadership has supports in Western Europe, and promoting parties with conservative and nationalist values.[13]

Russia also has close links to various Western European far-left parties. Such influence can be seen as a remnant of Soviet-era relations with European communist parties, but it is also, to some extent, in line with Russia's interest in supporting far-right parties. Both ends of

---

she also met with Deputy Prime Minister Dmitry Rogozin (cited by Paul Ames, "Europe's Far Right Is Embracing Putin," *Global Post*, April 10, 2014).

[9]   Grynszpan, 2013.

[10]   Suzanne Daley and Maïa de la Baume, "French Far Right Gets Helping Hand With Russian Loan," *New York Times*, December 1, 2014.

[11]   Péter Krekó, "The Russian Connection: The Spread of Pro-Russian Policies on the European Far Right," transcript of opening remarks, Forum 2000 Conference, Political Capital Institute, Prague, p. 6; Ames, 2014.

[12]   Vincent Jauvert, "Poutine et le FN: Révélations sur les Réseaux Russes des Le Pen," *Le Nouvel Observateur*, November 27, 2014.

[13]   Orenstein, 2014; Grynszpan, 2013; Alina Polyakova, "Strange Bedfellows: Putin and Europe's Far Right," *World Affairs*, September/October 2014, p. 37.

the political spectrum have common views that Moscow also shares, including an aversion to the European Union and an anti-American stance. An overwhelming proportion of those members of the European Parliament who voted against the ratification of the EU-Ukraine Association Agreement belonged to far-right and far-left parties.[14]

Could Pro-Russian Parties Influence EU Policy?

Another important motive for Putin's support to populist parties is to weaken the European Union while also seeking to gain some degree of influence on both the decisions made at the EU level and the organization's ability to reach such decisions. Gaining influence at the EU level may also enable Russia to have an impact on discussions regarding the European energy market, which it regards as being of key importance.

Far-right parties in Western Europe all agree in their opposition to the European Union.[15] The Ukrainian crisis has bolstered their rhetoric along two lines that dovetail with Putin's own discourse: (1) portraying the European Union as having a destabilizing influence, and (2) depicting the European Union as wasting money that could otherwise be better spent in countries still engulfed in the financial and economic crisis. The first theme has been endorsed in particular by Geert Wilders, who blamed the Ukrainian crisis on "shameless Europhiles with their dreams of empire," adding, "the EU stands for warmongering" in a March 2014 speech.[16] In another statement the following month, he blamed EU-Ukraine discussions on potential future integration as the cause of the crisis.[17] Leader of the United Kingdom

---

[14] Georgi Gotev, "Which MEPs Voted Against EU-Ukraine Association?" *Reuniting Europe* blog post, September 17, 2014. Based on data from VoteWatch Europe, "EU-Ukraine Association Agreement, with the Exception of the Treatment of Third Country Nationals Legally Employed as Workers in the Territory of the Other Party," September 16, 2014.

[15] Thomas Escritt and Anthony Deutsch, "Dutch Rightist Wilders Blames EU for Ukraine Crisis; Hints at UKIP Alliance," Reuters, April 17, 2014.

[16] Cited in Ames, 2014.

[17] Escritt and Deutsch, 2014.

Independence Party (UKIP) Nigel Farage stated that the European Union had "blood on its hands" for "destabilizing" Ukraine and called the EU foreign policy "disastrous."[18] In February 2014, Marine Le Pen claimed that the European Union had added fuel to the fire in Ukraine[19] and blamed it for declaring a "Cold War" on Russia during a visit to Moscow two months later.[20] Anti-Americanism and, more specifically, the idea that the European Union is an empty shell waging a war for its American master is also a common theme in statements and pronouncements by the far-right and far-left parties.[21] At a conference on EU-Russia relations organized by the European Parliament far-right parties, the leader of the Austrian party FPÖ decried Brussels as "playing the stooge of the U.S. in the encirclement of Russia."[22] Since France's return as a full participant in NATO's integrated command in 2009, the National Front has advocated undoing that move.[23]

In the 2014 EU parliamentary elections, populist parties obtained historically high scores in several countries (see Table 1 for far-right parties that came in third position or better in their respective countries).[24] The National Front in France, the Danish People's Party in Denmark, and UKIP in the United Kingdom all came in first place.

However, the significance of these results should not be overestimated. Voter turnout was low (43 percent),[25] as it always is in European

---

[18] "Farage: EU Does Have 'Blood on Its Hands' over Ukraine," BBC, March 27, 2014.

[19] Agence France-Presse, "L'UE a Jeté 'de l'Huile sur le Feu' en Ukraine et la France n'a Plus de Rôle à Jouer (Marine Le Pen)," February 20, 2014.

[20] Russian news agency Interfax, cited by Reuters (Alessandra Prentice, "France's Le Pen, in Moscow, Blames EU for New 'Cold War'," Reuters, April 12, 2014).

[21] Polyakova, 2014, p. 38.

[22] Cited in Charles Hawley, "'A Partner For Russia:' Europe's Far Right Flirts With Moscow," *Spiegel*, April 14, 2014.

[23] Licourt, 2014.

[24] It is worth noting that a number of parties critical of the European Union but not on the far right (e.g., Alternative für Deutschland in Germany, Beppe Grillo's Five Star Movement in Italy) also obtained good results.

[25] European Parliament, "Results of the 2014 European Elections: European Results," July 1, 2014.

Table 5.1
Success of Far-Right Parties in European
Parliament Elections (2014)

Country	Party	Position	% Votes
Denmark	Dansk Folkeparti	1	26.6
France	Front National	1	24.9
UK	UKIP	1	26.8
Austria	FPÖ	3	19.7
Netherlands	PVV	3	13.3

SOURCE: European Parliament, "Results of the 2014
European Parliament Elections: Results by Country,"
July 1, 2014.

elections, and the European Parliament is an institution perceived by European voters as being of marginal importance.[26] European elections have also been traditionally used in Europe as "protest" elections, precisely because they are perceived as being of limited political consequence. At the national level, most of these populist parties are still some way from acceding to power, where they would have a decisive impact on foreign policy decisions. In the meantime, their pro-Russian stance will play only a marginal role in most of their respective countries' political debate. Not only does foreign policy represent a marginal part of their programs (and their audiences' concerns), but their nationalistic programs also prevent them from too fully embracing Russian interests without losing credit with their supporters.

At the EU level, these parties' overall small number of representatives when compared with mainstream parties generally makes it unlikely that they can impose a dissenting view, although they can skew the debate. They also present very different—and hardly reconcilable—views on a number of issues. The People's Party in Denmark has been very critical of the National Front and Golden Dawn in Greece.[27]

---

[26] Polyakova, 2014, p. 40; Anne Applebaum, "A Tale of Two Europes," *Slate*, May 30, 2014.

[27] Harriet Alexander, "EU Elections 2014: Danish Eurosceptic People's Party Wins—And Calls for Alliance With Cameron," *Telegraph*, May 26, 2014.

UKIP's leader, Nigel Farage, has sought to distance his party from the National Front.[28] These parties also differ on the degree to which they are in accord with Moscow. While the National Front embraces Putin's political and social conservatism, Geert Wilders portrays himself as a defender of gay rights.[29] Wilders also has been described as pro–United States.[30] Nigel Farage has expressed his admiration for Putin "as an operator, but not as a human being."[31] Interestingly, neither UKIP nor the Dutch Freedom Party took part in the trip to Crimea to observe the referendum.[32] Yet, Marine Le Pen's ability to create a group at the European Parliament (named Europe of Nations and Freedom) in June 2015 suggests that these groups can unite, albeit with difficulty—it took the joining of one UKIP dissident and two members of Polish extreme-right party Congress of the New Right (KNP) for the group to be created.[33] The group is co-led by the National Front and PVV and also includes Austria's Freedom Party, Italy's Lega Nord, and Belgium's Vlaams Belang. Importantly, it will receive $20 million in funding over four years and provide its members additional speaking time and an increased ability to lead committees.[34] It is unclear yet whether this group will take an aggressive pro-Russian stance or will focus its action on the topics that most appeal to members' national audiences, such as immigration, security, or employment. It is also important to note that this group (36 members of Parliament) remains small in comparison to the heavyweights of the European Parliament—the Christian

---

[28] Alex Massie, "High Tea With a Spot of Racism," *Foreign Policy*, May 12, 2014.

[29] Polyakova, 2014, p. 40.

[30] Carol Matlack, "Why Europe's Far Right Is Getting Cozy with Russia," *Bloomberg Businessweek*, April 24, 2014.

[31] Interview of Nigel Farage with *GQ* Magazine quoted in "Nigel Farage: I Admire Vladimir Putin," *Guardian*, March 31, 2014.

[32] Matlack, 2014.

[33] Political groups require at least 25 members of Parliament from at least seven different countries.

[34] Henry Samuel and Matthew Holehouse, "Marine Le Pen Forms Far-Right Group in European Parliament," *Telegraph*, June 16, 2015; Alissa J. Rubin, "Far-Right Parties Form Coalition in European Parliament," *New York Times*, June 16, 2015.

Democrats group, for instance, includes almost 30 percent of all EU members of Parliament.[35]

Anti-EU parties will likely be emboldened by the victory of the British exit from the European Union ("Brexit"), heavily supported by UKIP, in the June 23, 2016 referendum that marks the first time an EU member chose to leave the Union. The ability of the United Kingdom to secure favorable bilateral agreements with the European Union and other nations, including the United States, as well as the overall effect of this decision on the British economy, will likely affect other EU members' willingness to remain in the Union—particularly for countries where anti-EU parties are particularly strong. At the same time, assuming Brexit occurs, the European Union will lose an influential voice for close transatlantic relations within its inner councils.

The Challenge of Maintaining European Unity on Russia Policy

Fault Lines on Russia in Northern and Central Europe

The Ukrainian crisis has exposed several fault lines on Russia policy across Europe. The first is between Northern and Central Europe. Estonia, Latvia, Lithuania, and Poland have called for a robust response to Russian aggression.[36] Poland and Lithuania have been in the forefront of those states arguing that the Ukrainian crisis is not a passing crisis but a permanent change in Russia's foreign policy that has major implications for Northern and Central Europe. By contrast, Hungary, the Czech Republic, and Slovakia have taken a more cautious and reserved approach that gives precedence to economic and energy interests. All three have expressed doubts about the impact of Western sanctions on Russian policy, arguing that the sanctions damage their own econo-

---

[35] Rubin, 2015.

[36] For a detailed discussion of the impact of the Ukrainian crisis on Central and Eastern Europe, see Joerg Forbrig, ed., "A Region Disunited? Central European Responses to the Russia-Ukraine Crisis," Europe Policy Paper 1, Washington, D.C.: The German Marshall Fund of the United States, February 2015.

mies more than Russia's economy. All three also have political features that may present vulnerabilities in case of continued Russian assertiveness, including populist parties that are political chameleons, personality politics, and small parties that may be critical to a government coalition.[37]

Fault Lines on Russia in Southeastern Europe

Additional fault lines exist in southeastern Europe. Bulgaria, Serbia, Greece, Cyprus, and Turkey have pursued friendly policies toward Russia. However, the motivations for their pro-Russian policies and extent of their vulnerability to Russian pressure and influence vary.

Bulgaria has strong historical and cultural ties to Russia going back to the late 19th century. During the Soviet period, political and economic ties were so close that Bulgaria was often jokingly referred to as the 16th Soviet Republic. Sofia remains highly dependent on Russia economically, especially for gas. (Bulgaria imports 90 percent of its natural gas from Russia.) This high dependency on Russian gas gives Moscow considerable leverage over Sofia's economy and ability to pursue a balanced foreign policy.

In addition, Russia retains close ties to many political groups and networks in Bulgaria from the Soviet period, including contacts with right-wing extremist forces such as Ataka. The leader of Ataka, Volen Siderov, has close ties to the Kremlin and received the Fatherland Star medal for his efforts to promote closer Bulgarian-Russian relations.[38] Russia also has strong links to the Bulgarian intelligence services—a carryover from the Soviet period. These networks have enabled Moscow to influence Bulgarian domestic and foreign policy.

However, Bulgaria has recently taken steps to reduce its dependence on Russian energy. The United States is working with officials in Sofia and Athens to establish a pipeline to Bulgaria from an LNG terminal in Greece. U.S. officials are also discussing diversifying Bul-

---

[37] These populist parties include Jobbik, in Hungary, and Action of Dissatisfied Citizens and Dawn of Direct Democracy in the Czech Republic.

[38] See Jim Yardley and Jo Becker, "How Putin Forged a Pipeline Deal That Derailed," *New York Times*, December 30, 2014.

garia's nuclear energy options, including a possible project in which Westinghouse Electric Company would build a nuclear power plant in Bulgaria.[39]

Russia has also sought to strengthen ties to Serbia. As in Bulgaria, Putin has relied on "crony capitalism" to expand Russia's economic and political ties with Serbia. The Russian Railways company, headed by Putin ally Vladimir Yakunin, is currently refurbishing a 350-km stretch of track in Serbia at a cost of three-quarters of a billion euros.[40] Russian investment has focused in particular on the energy sector in Serbia. Lukoil owns 79.5 percent of the local service station chain Beopetrol, while Gazprom has majority ownership of Serbia's natural gas supplier.[41] According to Eurostat data, in 2012, Serbia imported 100 percent of its natural gas either directly from Russia or as reimports of Russian gas via Hungary.

Putin's visit to Belgrade in October 2014 to celebrate the 70th anniversary of the liberation of Belgrade may signal a new, more active phase in Russian policy toward Serbia. The Serbian leadership rolled out the red carpet for Putin, hosting the largest military parade since 1986 in his honor.[42] While in Belgrade, Putin stressed the common Slav culture binding the two countries and the strong historical ties between Serbia and Russia. He also expressed strong support for Serbian policy toward Kosovo.

Russia has also made important inroads in Cyprus, a member of the EU since 2004. Cyprus has become an important tax haven and vehicle for money laundering and other criminal activities by Russian tycoons and businessmen. Huge sums of Russian money are invested in Cyprus, much of it dirty money repatriated back to Russia. This has the effect of making Russia, on paper, one of the largest investors in Cyprus worldwide. Cyprus's growing economic and cultural ties to

---

[39] Michael R. Gordon, "U.S. to help Bulgaria Depend Less on Russians," *New York Times*, January 15, 2015.

[40] Gordon, 2015.

[41] Gordon, 2015.

[42] Neil Buckley and Andrew Byrne, "Serbia's Grand Welcome for Putin Likely to Jar with West," *Financial Times*, October 15, 2014.

Russia have raised concerns in Brussels. EU officials fear that these growing economic ties between Cyprus and Russia could give Moscow a potential means of influencing Cypriot policy, particularly regarding future contracts for the natural gas reserves currently under exploration off the Cypriot coast.

However, Russia's prospects for influencing Greek policy have declined. The settlement of Greece's debt problems strengthens EU influence over Greece's economy and ends whatever hope Russia may have had of exploiting Greece's economic difficulties for its own political advantage.

Finally, Turkey is emerging as an important factor in the Russian-European equation because of its growing economic interaction with Russia. Historically, Russia and Turkey have been bitter enemies. Over the past several centuries, they have fought 13 wars against each other, most of which Turkey lost. This historical animosity was reinforced by Stalin's aggressive policy toward Turkey early in the Cold War, the driving force behind Turkey's decision to join NATO in 1952. In the past decade, however, Turkey's relations with Russia have improved markedly, especially in the economic realm. Energy has been a major driver of the improvement in relations. Russia is Turkey's largest trading partner and its largest supplier of natural gas, supplying more than 50 percent of Turkey's natural gas and 40 percent of its crude oil.

Yet, Turkey is unlikely to add another fault line in southeastern Europe on attitudes toward Russia. Turkish and Russian interests conflict in a number of areas, particularly the Caucasus (a region in which Turkey has deep and long-standing strategic interests) and, to a lesser extent, Central Asia. Turkish and Russian policy toward Syria is another area where the interests of the two countries largely conflict. Turkey has sought Syrian President Bashar al-Assad's overthrow, while Russia is one of Assad's strongest supporters.

Turkey and Russia are also energy competitors in the Caspian region. Russia wants to control the distribution and export lines of energy resources in those regions and has opposed such schemes as the (now defunct) Nabucco and Transcaspian pipelines, projects that would provide alternative means for exporting the region's energy resources to Europe. Turkey, however, hopes to become a hub for the transport of natural gas to Europe.

In short, while Turkish-Russian relations have significantly improved in the past decade, the strategic interests of the two countries conflict in important areas, including toward Syria and the Kurds whose struggle for independence Moscow has off and on supported when it suited its strategic interest. These conflicting interests are likely to prevent any long-lasting and fundamental realignment of Turkish-Russian relations.

Fault Lines on Russia in Western Europe

Public opinion polls in Germany show that the German public is divided regarding relations with Russia. In March 2014, polling indicated that about a third of Germans and French opposed imposing trade sanctions on Russia (while 23 percent of British respondents did).[43] A survey by *Der Spiegel* showed that 55 percent of Germans had "a lot" or "some" sympathy for Putin's views that Crimea is part of Russia.[44] German views shifted toward supporting sanctions after the downing of Malaysian Airlines Flight 17 over Ukraine in July 2014,[45] but in November 2014, 39 percent of German respondents "mostly agree[d]" that Germany should "accept the Russian annexation of Crimea, and endorse this decision legally."[46] As of early 2015, most

---

[43] YouGov, "Survey Results," poll conducted among northwestern European adults, March 21–27, 2014.

[44] *Der Spiegel* survey conducted by TNS Forschung with 1,000 Germans on March 19–20, 2014 Spiegel Online International, "Spiegel Survey on the Crimea Crisis," TNS Forschung, March 19–20 2014.

[45] An Infratest Dimap poll conducted in August 2014 showed 70 percent of German respondents agreeing that "the EU is right to respond with sanctions." Infratest Dimap/ARD poll conducted on August 4–5, 2014, and cited in Harriet Torry, "Germans Back Tougher Stance Toward Russia Over Ukraine—Poll," *Wall Street Journal*, August 8, 2014.

[46] Infratest Dimap poll cited in Rick Noack, "Why Do Nearly 40 Percent of Germans Endorse Russia's Annexation of Crimea?" *Washington Post*, November 28, 2014.

Germans, however, approved of sanctions—65 percent in February, up from 54 percent in December 2014.[47]

German elites appear divided on the sanctions issue, with more than 60 personalities from politics, economy, culture, and media writing an open letter in December 2014 entitled, "Another War in Europe? Not in Our Name!" that called for a "new policy of détente for Europe,"[48] while another hundred or so academics and journalists published another letter ("Do Not Reward Expansionism") arguing the opposite.[49] A poll carried out on March 10–14, 2014, in France and Germany showed that 62 percent of German respondents and 71 percent of French respondents were opposed to Ukraine joining the European Union.[50]

France has also shown some reluctance to damage relations with Russia. In a January 2015 poll for *La Tribune*, 80 percent agreed with the statement that "Economic relations with Russia have great importance for the French economy."[51] In addition, the European Union's role in the Ukraine crisis is seen in France with a certain degree of suspicion. In a December 2014 poll, 50 percent of respondents considered that Ukraine was first and foremost an area of political and economic interest for Russia, while only 19 percent saw it first and foremost as an area of political and economic interest for the European Union.[52] French attitudes toward Russia are further complicated by the con-

---

[47] Infratest Dimap, "ARD DeutschlandTREND February 2015," survey results, 2015, p. 7. Poll was conducted on February 2–3, 2015, with 1,003 respondents.

[48] "Wieder Krieg in Europa? Nicht in Unserem Namen!" *Zeit* Online, December 5, 2014.

[49] Paul Roderick Gregory, "The Battle for German Public Opinion: The Russia/Ukraine Narrative," *Forbes*, December 15, 2015.

[50] Ifop poll for *Le Figaro*, cited in Alain Barluet, "Français et Allemands Hostiles à l'Entrée de l'Ukraine dans l'UE," *Le Figaro*, March 14, 2014. This figure went down for France to 63 percent in a December 2014 poll (BVA poll for *Ukraine Today*, "Enquête d'Opinion Auprès des Français sur l'Ukraine," conducted on December 10 and 11, 2014, with 1,176 respondents.)

[51] Ifop poll for *La Tribune*, "Les Français, la Perception du Conflit Ukraino-Russe et la Livraison de Navires de Guerre à la Russie," conducted from January 9 through 12, 2015, with 1,001 respondents, p. 6.

[52] 29 percent of respondents answered that Ukraine was neither.

troversy over the delivery of the two Mistral-class amphibious assault ships sold to Russia in 2011 that were due to be delivered in 2014 and 2015. Sixty-four percent of French respondents in a January 2015 poll stated that France should deliver the ships to Russia, while 36 percent opposed it. Seventy-five percent of respondents thought that withholding delivery would be "not effective" in helping resolve the conflict in Ukraine.[53]

It remains to be seen whether the ambivalent attitude of the French public toward sanctions against Russia will have a serious influence on the position of France's political leaders. French President François Hollande has maintained his policy of not delivering the Mistral ships to Russia, in spite of the economic costs that this will entail for France (an estimated billion euros, before potential penalties that might follow if Russia decides to take the matter to court).[54] However, he publicly expressed his discontent with the sanctions in January 2015, stating that risks of further Russian expansionism are limited: "What Mr. Putin wants is that Ukraine not become a member of NATO."[55] That same month, German Vice-Chancellor and Minister for Economic Affairs and Energy Sigmar Gabriel and Foreign Minister Frank-Walter Steinmeier also expressed strong reservations regarding the imposition of sanctions against Russia.[56]

So far, these ambivalent attitudes have not resulted in a major breakdown of EU solidarity on the sanctions issue—largely thanks to the firm leadership of Chancellor Angela Merkel of Germany, who pushed hard for a toughening of the sanctions after the shooting down of the Malaysian commercial airliner MH 17 in July 2014. Without her

---

[53] Ifop, 2015, pp. 10–11.

[54] This includes the reimbursement to Russia of what it has already paid; late delivery penalties; and the monthly cost of keeping the ships in a French harbor (Jean-Dominique Merchet, "Exclusif: La Non-Livraison du Mistral Coûtera 5 Millions par Mois à la France, *L'Opinion*, February 12, 2015.).

[55] Cited in Andrew E. Kramer, "French Leader Urges End to Sanctions Against Russia over Ukraine," *New York Times*, January 5, 2015.

[56] Jack Ewing and Alison Smale, "In Reversal, Germany Cools to Russian Investment," *New York Times*, December 28, 2014.

principled leadership, the sanctions would have been much weaker and might not have been imposed at all. Merkel had initially hoped that she could nudge Putin along toward a diplomatic solution. But after the shooting down of the Malaysian commercial airliner, Merkel lost trust in Putin because she believed that he had repeatedly lied to her about Russia's involvement and support for the separatists.[57]

Whether the sanctions are eased or even expanded will depend heavily on Russian policy and behavior. Collapse of the Minsk II agreement and/or a push by the separatists to expand the territory they currently occupy could have a serious impact on EU policy and public support for the sanctions. Germany's attitude will be critical. Many European leaders will be watching Merkel closely to see how she manages the sanctions issue at home and follow suit.

Conclusion

In spite of the many fault lines over Russia policy that exist in Europe, as well as the growing influence, both nationally and at the EU level, of populist parties that offer (more often than not) pro-Russian views, EU members have voted overall to pursue economic sanctions unanimously every time they came up for renewal. This should not obscure the fact that several countries have expressed doubts about the ability of sanctions to change Russian policy, and concerns regarding the impact of sanctions and countersanctions on their own economies. As mentioned earlier, such countries include Hungary, the Czech Republic, and Slovakia, as well as Greece and Italy. Yet, reservations from these countries have not compromised EU unanimity on this topic. President of the EU Council Donald Tusk has played an important role in maintaining consensus on this matter among the 28, through consultations and negotiations that are, when needed, supplemented by

---

[57] See Quentin Peel, "Merkel Wants a Stable World and Is Willing to Pay a Price for it," *Financial Times*, August 12, 2014. Also, Stefan Wagstyl, "Merkel Rethink on Tough Action Reflects Loss of Trust in Putin," *Financial Times,* July 17, 2014.

diplomatic activity from powerful EU players such as Germany.[58] As two journalists put it, "smaller nations may be loath to defy Berlin."[59] Dissenting countries also generally stand to lose more by breaking ranks with the European Union than they would gain by bringing the sanctions to a halt.[60]

---

[58] Face-to-face and phone interviews with EU officials, June 2015.

[59] Peter Baker and Steven Erlanger, "Russia Uses Money and Ideology to Fight Western Sanctions," *New York Times*, June 7, 2015.

[60] See, for instance, Denis Dyomkin, "Putin Visits Italy with One Eye on EU Sanctions," Reuters, June 9, 2015.

CHAPTER SIX

Conclusion

European countries differ widely in how vulnerable they are to possible Russian actions. Whereas the states in southern or western parts of Europe have some economic vulnerability and might suffer some temporary disruptions from economic sanctions imposed on or by Russia, the EU/NATO states in Northern and Central Europe have greater exposure to Russian actions because of their proximity to Russia, their history of recent domination by the Soviet Union, and, in some cases, the continuing legacies of the Soviet empire. Of these countries, only Estonia, Latvia, and, to a lesser degree, Lithuania face a serious conventional military threat, even though their neighbors—Poland, Sweden, and Finland—also feel a growing degree of vulnerability. And, of course, Europe and the United States remain vulnerable to Russian nuclear forces, as Russia does to American, French, and British nuclear forces.

Europe offers little vulnerability to Russian economic pressures. It bears repeating that only about 1 percent of the European Union's total nonenergy imports came from Russia in 2013.[1] European needs in almost all sectors can be readily covered by other suppliers. It is true that a small subset of European countries—Lithuania, Finland, Estonia, Poland, and Norway—has been disproportionately affected by Russian countersanctions on agricultural and fishery products when

---

[1] In 2013, the EU28 imported about 3.7 trillion euros of nonenergy goods, of which only 46.3 billion euros' worth were imports from Russia. This 46.3 billion euros of nonenergy imports represented 22 percent of all Russian goods traded to the European Union (Eurostat, undated).

compared with other European countries, but these countries have also shown strong resolve against Russia, suggesting resilience in the face of economic losses. Advanced European economies, first and foremost Germany, also have been suffering a slowdown in export-led growth in many nonagricultural industries, such as manufacturing, automobiles, chemicals, and machinery, because of the fall in Russian purchasing power and access to credit, but so far this has had limited impact on Germany's broader economy.

It is also important to note that the relation of dependency between Europe and Russia works both ways, creating vulnerabilities on the Russian side as well—vulnerabilities currently targeted by sanctions. Europe invests more in Russia than Russia invests in Europe. Europe relies on Russia for a not-insignificant share of its energy, but Russia relies on Western European technology and capital for its oil exploration and extraction industries. Trade relations with Russia are particularly important for some European countries, such as Germany, but they are also important for Russia: Europe is Russia's most important source of imports. These Russian vulnerabilities will be examined further in a subsequent report in this series.

Although Russia provides a high percentage of European oil supplies, Russia's oil exports provide it with little leverage. If Russia were to halt oil exports to Europe, Europe could easily import oil from other suppliers. We also found the European Union to be less vulnerable to interruptions in the flow of Russian gas than is generally perceived. Although Russia is the largest single supplier of gas to EU member states, they also import gas large quantities from Algeria, Norway, and, more recently, LNG from Qatar and other suppliers. Domestic production also covers a substantial share of consumption. In our view, increased imports of LNG, fuel substitution, and efficiency measures should be adequate to compensate for a permanent cutoff in Russian gas, although at some economic cost. However, the smaller economies of southeastern, northeastern, and Central Europe are vulnerable to a cutoff in Russian natural gas supplies. In some instances these countries are taking measures, such as building liquefied gas terminals, to reduce these vulnerabilities. In other cases, they would need to rely on transshipments of natural gas from Western Europe.

Finally, Russia can try to exploit the political vulnerabilities of a number of countries. In the Baltic states, it could try to manipulate the Russian minorities issue to stir discontent in Latvia and Estonia. Russia could also attempt to influence Baltic states politics from the inside, by infiltrating some political parties, or from the outside, by creating a situation whereby some Western government may try to pressure Latvia and Estonia to provide more favorable policies toward their minorities—potentially damaging relations between Western and northeastern Europe and stirring more discontent within the latter. In the rest of Europe, populist parties are on the rise and have often adopted pro-Russian stances. In spite of the many fault lines that exist across Europe on Russian policy, the EU consensus on sanctions toward Russia was still holding as of late 2016.

References

Abdelal, Rawi, "The Profits of Power: Commerce and Realpolitik in Eurasia," *Review of International Political Economy*, Vol. 20, No. 3, 2013, pp. 421–456.

Abramov, Denis, "How Sanctions Against Russia Have Affected European Companies," *Moscow Times,* August 7, 2014.

Agence France-Presse, "L'UE a Jeté 'de l'Huile sur le Feu' en Ukraine et la France n'a Plus de Rôle à Jouer (Marine Le Pen)," February 20, 2014.

Alexander, Harriet, "EU Elections 2014: Danish Eurosceptic People's Party Wins—and Calls for Alliance with Cameron," *Telegraph,* May 26, 2014.

Ames, Paul, "Europe's Far Right Is Embracing Putin," *GlobalPost,* April 10, 2014.

Applebaum, Anne, "A Tale of Two Europes," *Slate,* May 30, 2014.

Baker, Peter, and Steven Erlanger, "Russia Uses Money and Ideology to Fight Western Sanctions," *New York Times,* June 7, 2015. As of February 23, 2016: http://www.nytimes.com/2015/06/08/world/europe/ russia-fights-wests-ukraine-sanctions-with-aid-and-ideology.html?_r=0

Barluet, Alain, "Français et Allemands Hostiles à l'Entrée de l'Ukraine dans l'UE." *Le Figaro,* March 14, 2014. As of February 23, 2016: http://www.lefigaro.fr/international/2014/03/14/01003-20140314ARTFIG00358- francais-et-allemands-hostiles-a-l-entree-de-l-ukraine-dans-l-ue.php?pagination=7

Barno, David, and Nora Bensahel, "The Anti-Access Challenge You're Not Thinking About," *War on the Rocks,* May 5, 2015. As of February 23, 2016: http://warontherocks.com/2015/05/ the-anti-access-challenge-youre-not-thinking-about/

Berzina, Ieva, ed., "The Possiblity of Societal Destabilization in Latvia: Potential National Security Threats, Executive Summary of the Research Report," Riga, Latvia, Center for Security and Strategic Research, National Defence Academy of Latvia, 2016.

Bray, Chad, "European Banks Expect Only 'Limited' Impact from Sanctions on Russia," *New York Times,* August 21, 2014.

Breedlove, Philip M., "Transcript: After the Summit, General Philip M. Breedlove on NATO's Path Forward," Washington, D.C., Atlantic Council, September 19, 2014.

Brzezinksi, Ian J., and Nicholas Varangis, "The NATO-Russia Exercise Gap," Washington, D.C., Atlantic Council, February 23, 2015. As of June 19, 2015: http://www.atlanticcouncil.org/blogs/natosource/the-nato-russia-exercise-gap.

Buckley, Edgar, and Ioan Pascu, "NATO's Article 5 and Russian Hybrid Warfare," March 17, 2015. As of June 19, 2015: http://www.atlanticcouncil.org/blogs/natosource/ nato-s-article-5-and-russian-hybrid-warfare

Buckley, Neil, and Andrew Byrne, "Serbia's Grand Welcome for Putin Likely to Jar with West," *Financial Times,* October 16, 2011.

BVA, "Enquête d'Opinion Auprès des Français sur l'Ukraine," survey conducted for *Ukraine Today,* January 2015. As of June 19, 2015: http://www.bva.fr/data/sondage/sondage_fiche/1645/fichier_bva_-_enquete_ dopinion_aupres_des_francais_sur_lukraine_-_decembre_2014fc742.pdf

Byrne, Andrew, and Christian Oliver, "Brussels Veto of Hungarian Nuclear Deal Set to Inflame Tensions with Russia," *Financial Times,* March 13, 2015.

Colby, Elbridge, *Nuclear Weapons in the Third Offset Strategy: Avoiding a Nuclear Blind Spot in the Pentagon's New Initiative,* Washington, D.C.: Center for a New American Security, January 2015.

Collins, James F., Ross A. Virginia, and Kenneth Yalowitz, "Hands Across the Melting Ice," *New York Times,* May 13, 2013. As of June 19, 2015: http://www.nytimes.com/2013/05/14/opinion/global/ Hands-Across-the-Melting-Arctic.html?_r=0

Crane, Keith, Andreas Goldthau, Michael Toman, Thomas Light, Stuart E. Johnson, Alireza Nader, Angel Rabasa, and Harun Dogo, *Imported Oil and U.S. National Security,* Santa Monica, Calif.: RAND Corporation, MG-838-USCC, 2009. As of February 23, 2016: http://www.rand.org/pubs/monographs/MG838.html

Daley, Suzanne, and Maïa de la Baume, "French Far Right Gets Helping Hand With Russian Loan," *New York Times,* December 1, 2014. As of June 19, 2015: http://www.nytimes.com/2014/12/02/world/europe/ french-far-right-gets-helping-hand-with-russian-loan-.html

Dickel, Ralf, Elham Hassanzadeh, James Henderson, Anouk Honoré, Laura El-Katiri, Simon Pirani, Howard Rogers, Jonathan Stern, and Katja Yafimava, "Reducing European Dependence on Russian Gas: Distinguishing Natural Gas Security from Geopolitics," OIES Paper: NG 92, Oxford, UK: Oxford Institute for Energy Studies, University of Oxford, October 2014, p. 1.

Dyomkin, Denis, "Putin Visits Italy with One Eye on EU Sanctions," Reuters, June 9, 2015. As of September 17, 2015:
http://www.reuters.com/article/2015/06/10/
us-italy-russia-idUSKBN0OP2EA20150610

Energy Information Administration, "Norway," web page, U.S. Department of Energy, April 28, 2014. As of August 27, 2015:
http://www.eia.gov/countries/cab.cfm?fips=no

Escritt, Thomas, and Anthony Deutsch, *Dutch Rightist Wilders Blames EU for Ukraine Crisis; Hints at UKIP Alliance,* Reuters, April 17, 2014.

European Chemical Site Promotion Platform, *An Overview of the Pipeline Networks of Europe,* undated. As of September 17, 2015:
https://chemicalparks.eu/system/files/attachments/file/14/
European_Pipeline_Infrastructure__Networks.pdf

European Commission, "Communication from the Commission to the European Parliament and the Council on the Short Term Resilience of the European Gas System: Preparedness for a Possible Disruption of Supplies from the East During the Fall and Winter of 2014/2015," SWD(2014) 322 Final, Brussels, October 16, 2014.

European Parliament, "Results of the 2014 European Elections: European Results," July 1, 2014.

Eurostat, "Energy Balances," database, undated. As of September 17, 2015:
http://ec.europa.eu/eurostat/web/energy/data/energy-balances

Ewing, Jack, and Alison Smale, "In Reversal, Germany Cools to Russian Investment," *New York Times,* December 28, 2014.

Faiola, Anthony, "From Russia with Love: An Energy Deal for Hungary," *Washington Post,* February 16, 2015.

"Farage: EU Does Have 'Blood on its Hands' over Ukraine," BBC News, March 27, 2014.

Fingrid, "Power System in Finland," website, undated. As of September 17, 2015:
http://www.fingrid.fi/en/powersystem/general%20description/
Power%20System%20in%20Finland/Pages/default.aspx

Fisher, Max, "Why One of Russia's Top Foreign Policy Experts Is Worried About a Major War with Europe," *Vox,* May 6, 2015. As of September 17, 2015:
http://www.vox.com/2015/5/6/8540063/russia-europe-war

Foeger, Leonhard, "Gazprom, BASF Abandon Multibillion Dollar Energy Asset Swap," Reuters, December 19, 2014.

Forbrig, Joerg, ed., "A Region Disunited? Central European Responses to the Russia-Ukraine Crisis," Europe Policy Paper 1, Washington, D.C.: The German Marshall Fund of the United States, February 2015.

Fox, Benjamin, "Russia Invites EU Far-Right To Observe Crimea Vote," *EU Observer,* March 13, 2014.

Gazprom Export, "Delivery Statistics: Gas Supplies to Europe," fact sheet, undated.

Geiger, Friedrich, "German Exports to Russia Fall off Further as Sanctions Take Hold: New Data Shows Sharp Decline," *Wall Street Journal,* October 29, 2014.

Gibbs, Walter, "Russia and Norway Reach Accord on Barents Sea," *New York Times,* April 27, 2010.

Gorenburg, Dmitry, "Countering Color Revolutions: Russia's New Security Strategy and Its Implications for U.S. Policy," *Russian Military Reform,* September 2014. As of February 24, 2016:
https://russiamil.wordpress.com/2014/09/15/countering-color-revolutions-russias-new-security-strategy-and-its-implications-for-u-s-policy/

Gorst, Isabel, "Construction of Tanap Pipeline Begins in Turkey as EU and Russia Spar for Upper Hand," *Financial Times,* March 18, 2015.

Gotev, Georgi, "Which MEPs Voted Against EU-Ukraine Association?" *Reuniting Europe* blog post, September 17, 2014.

Gregory, Paul R., "The Battle for German Public Opinion: The Russia/Ukraine Narrative," *Forbes,* December 15, 2015. As of February 24, 2016:
http://www.forbes.com/sites/paulroderickgregory/2014/12/15/the-battle-for-german-public-opinion-the-russiaukraine-narrative

Grove, Thomas, "Russia Starts Nationwide Show of Force," Reuters, March 16, 2015. As of September 17, 2015:
http://www.reuters.com/article/2015/03/16/us-russia-military-exercises-idUSKBN0MC0JO20150316

Grynszpan, Emmanuel, "Moscou Déroule le Tapis Rouge Devant Marine Le Pen," *Le Figaro,* June 20, 2013.

Hadjipapas, Andreas, "Cyprus Nears €2.5bn Russian Loan Deal," *Financial Times,* September 14, 2011.

Hawley, Charles, "'A Partner for Russia': Europe's Far Right Flirts with Moscow," *Spiegel,* April 14, 2014.

Higgins, Andrew, "Far-Right Fever for a Europe Tied to Russia," *New York Times,* May 20, 2014.

"How to Deal with Harmony," *Economist,* October 6, 2014.

Ifop, "Les Français, la Perception du Conflit Ukraino-Russe et la Livraison de Navires de Guerre à la Russie," survey conducted for *La Tribune,* January 2015. As of February 23, 2016:
http://www.ifop.com/media/poll/2912-1-study_file.pdf

IMF—*See* International Monetary Fund.

Infratest Dimap, "ARD DeutschlandTREND Februar 2015," survey results, 2015. As of February 23, 2016:
http://www.infratest-dimap.de/uploads/media/2015.02.05_DT1502_bericht.pdf

Innes, Abby, "Hungary's Illiberal Democracy," *Current History*, Vol. 114, No. 770, March 2015.

International Energy Agency, Statistics, web page, undated. As of September 17, 2015:
http://www.iea.org/statistics/

International Group of Liquefied Natural Gas Importers, *The LNG Industry, 2013*, Neuilly-sur-Seine, France: GIIGNL, 2013, p. 13. As of September 17, 2015:
http://www.giignl.org/

International Institute for Strategic Studies, "The Military Balance 2015," Chapters 4 and 5, February 2015.

International Monetary Fund, "Russian Federation: Staff Report for the 2014 Article IV Consultation," IMF Country Report No. 14/175, Washington, D.C., June 11, 2014.

Interview of Nigel Farage with GQ Magazine, quoted in "Nigel Farage: I Admire Vladimir Putin," *Guardian*, March 31, 2014.

Jauvert, Vincent, "Poutine et le FN: Révélations sur les Réseaux Russes des Le Pen," *Nouvel Observateur*, November 27, 2014.

Jones, Bruce, "Russia Places 38,000 Troops on Alert for Snap Exercises," *Jane's Defence Weekly*, March 16, 2015.

Jones, Erik, "EU Sanctions Against Russia Are a Double-Edged Sword," *Moscow Times*, August 3, 2014.

Kivirähk, Juhan, "Integrating Estonia's Russian-Speaking Population: Findings of National Defense Opinion Surveys," International Centre for Defence and Security, December 2014. As of February 24, 2016:
http://www.icds.ee/fileadmin/media/icds.ee/failid/
Juhan_Kivirahk_-_Integrating_Estonias_Russian-Speaking_Population.pdf

Kramer, Andrew, "Russia Seeks Sanctions Tit for Tat," *New York Times,* October 8, 2014.

———, "French Leader Urges End to Sanctions Against Russia over Ukraine," *New York Times,* January 5, 2015.

Kramer, Mark, "The New Russian Chill in the Baltic," *Current History*, Vol. 114, No. 770, March 2015. As of February 24, 2016:
http://www.currenthistory.com/Article.php?ID=1228

Krekó, Péter, "The Russian Connection: The Spread of Pro-Russian Policies on the European Far Right," transcript of opening remarks, Forum 2000 Conference, Political Capital Institute, Prague, p. 6.

Licourt, Julien, "L'Indéfectible Soutien du FN à la Russie de Poutine," *Le Figaro*, March 19, 2014.

Massie, Alex, "High Tea with a Spot of Racism," *Foreign Policy*, May 12, 2014.

Matlack, Carol, "Why Europe's Far Right Is Getting Cozy with Russia," *Bloomberg Businessweek,* April 24, 2014 .

McLaughlin, Eliott C., "Amid NATO Exercises, Russia Puts Northern Fleet on Full Alert," CNN, March 17, 2015.

Merchet, Jean-Dominique, "Exclusif: La Non-Livraison du Mistral Coûtera 5 Millions par Mois à la France," *L'Opinion,* February 12, 2015. As of February 24, 2016:
http://www.lopinion.fr/blog/secret-defense/
exclusif-non-livraison-mistral-coutera-5-millions-mois-a-france-21286

"Merkel Pledges NATO Will Defend Baltic Member States," Reuters, August 18, 2014. As of February 24, 2016:
http://www.reuters.com/article/2014/08/18/
us-ukraine-crisis-baltics-merkel-idUSKBN0GI1JI20140818

Michta, Andrew A., "Putin Targets the Scandinavians," *American Interest,* November 17, 2014. As of February 24, 2016:
http://www.the-american-interest.com/2014/11/17/
putin-targets-the-scandinavians/

Milne, Richard, "Lundin Makes 'Game-Changer' Oil Discovery in Norwegian Arctic," *Financial Times*, October 14, 2014a. As of September 17, 2015:
http://www.ft.com/intl/cms/s/0/f60699f4-53a9-11e4-929b-html#axzz3LApFoE3f

———, "Lithuania to Complete Western Integration as Kremlin Rattles Baltics," *Financial Times*, December 30, 2014b.

———, "Party with Ties to Putin Pushes Ahead in Estonian Polls," *Financial Times,* February 27, 2015.

Milne, Richard, Sam Jones, and Kathrin Hille, "Russian Air Incursions Rattle Baltic States," *Financial Times*, September 24, 2014.

NATO—See North Atlantic Treaty Organization.

Neuger, James, "Is EU Support for Russia Sanctions Waning? See Who's Visiting the Kremlin," *BloombergBusiness*, March 17, 2015.

Neukirch, Ralf, "The Sympathy Problem: Is Germany a Country of Russia Apologists?" *Spiegel,* March 31, 2014. As of September 17, 2015:
http://www.spiegel.de/international/germany/prominent-germans-have-
understanding-for-russian-annexation-of-crimea-a-961711.html

Noack, Rick, "Why Do Nearly 40 Percent of Germans Endorse Russia's Annexation of Crimea?" *Washington Post,* November 28, 2014. As of September 17, 2015: http://www.washingtonpost.com/blogs/worldviews/wp/2014/11/28/why-do-nearly-40-percent-of-germans-endorse-russias-annexation-of-crimea/

Norman, Laurence, "EU Projects Impact of Sanctions on Russian Economy," *Wall Street Journal,* October 29, 2014.

North Atlantic Treaty Organization, "NATO's Readiness Action Plan," fact sheet, December 2014. As of September 17, 2015: http://www.nato.int/nato_static_fl2014/assets/pdf/pdf_2014_12/20141202_141202-facstsheet-rap-en.pdf

———, "NATO Allies Begin Naval Exercise BALTOPS in the Baltic Sea," website, June 20, 2015. As of February 28, 2016: http://www.nato.int/cps/en/natohq/news_120407.htm

———, "Warsaw Summit Communique," July 6, 2016. As of October 12, 2016 http://www.nato.int/cps/en/natohq/official_texts_133169.htm

Norwegian Ministry of Foreign Affairs, "Norway Tightens Restrictive Measures Against Russia," press release, October 10, 2014.

Oliker, Olga, Michael J. McNerney, and Lynn E. Davis, *NATO Needs a Comprehensive Strategy for Russia,* Santa Monica, Calif.: RAND Corporation, PE-143-OSD, 2015. As of February 25, 2016: http://www.rand.org/pubs/perspectives/PE143.html

"Orban Renews Autonomy Call for Ethnic Hungarians in Ukraine," Reuters, May 17, 2014.

Orenstein, Mitchell A., "Putin's Western Allies," *Foreign Affairs,* March 25, 2014.

Pellerin, Cheryl, "U.S. Troops Resuming Atlantic Resolve Training in Eastern Europe," DoD News, January 12, 2015. As of March 25, 2014: http://www.defense.gov/News-Article-View/Article/603910

Pifer, Steven, "NATO's Response Must Be Conventional Not Nuclear," *Survival,* Vol. 57, No. 2, April–May 2015.

Pindják, Peter, "Deterring Hybrid Warfare: A Chance for NATO and the EU to Work Together?" *NATO Review,* 2014. As of March 25, 2014: http://www.nato.int/docu/review/2014/also-in-2014/Deterring-hybrid-warfare/EN/index.htm

Podvig, Pavel, "Sorting Fact From Fiction on Russian Missile Claims," *Bulletin of the Atomic Scientists,* June 22, 2015.

Polyakova, Alina, "Strange Bedfellows: Putin and Europe's Far Right," *World Affairs,* September/October 2014, p. 37.

Prentice, Alessandra, "France's Le Pen, in Moscow, Blames EU for New 'Cold War'," Reuters, April 12, 2014.

President of Russia, "Voennaia Doktrina Rossiiskoi Federatsii," December 26, 2014. As of August 27, 2015:
http://kremlin.ru/events/president/news/47334

Quinlivan, James T., "Yes, Russia's Military Is Getting More Aggressive," *Foreign Policy*, December 30, 2014.

Quinlivan, James T., and Olga Oliker, *Nuclear Deterrence in Europe: Russian Approaches to a New Environment and Implications for the United States*, Santa Monica, Calif.: RAND Corporation, MG-1075-AF, 2011. As of February 25, 2016:
http://www.rand.org/pubs/monographs/MG1075.html

Rapoza, Kenneth, "Here's What Putin's Counter-Sanctions Did to EU Exporters," *Forbes*, April 17, 2015.

Razumovskaya, Olga, "Cyprus Signs Deal to Let Russian Navy Ships Stop at Its Ports," *Wall Street Journal,* February 25, 2015.

Rotenberg, Olga, "Greek PM Blasts Russia Sanctions at Putin Meet," Agence France-Presse, April 8, 2015. As of August 27, 2015:
http://news.yahoo.com/greek-pm-moscow-putin-meet-rattles-eu-032442672.html

Rubin, Alissa J., "Far-Right Parties Form Coalition in European Parliament," *New York Times*, June 16, 2015. As of August 27, 2015:
http://www.nytimes.com/2015/06/17/world/europe/far-right-parties-form-coalition-in-european-parliament.html

Samuel, Henry, and Matthew Holehouse, "Marine Le Pen Forms Far-Right Group in European Parliament," *Telegraph*, June 16, 2015. As of August 27, 2015:
http://www.telegraph.co.uk/news/worldnews/europe/france/11678565/Marine-Le-Pen-forms-far-Right-group-in-European-Parliament.html

Shemetov, Maxim, "Thriving BP Worried by Impact of Harsher Sanctions on Rosneft Ties," *Moscow Times*, July 29, 2014.

Shlapak, David A., and Michael W. Johnson, Reinforcing Deterrence on NATO's Eastern Flank: Wargaming the Defense of the Baltics, Santa Monica, Calif.: RAND Corporation, RR-1253-A, 2016. As of February 25, 2016:
http://www.rand.org/pubs/research_reports/RR1253.html

Sokov, Nikolai N., "Why Russia Calls a Limited Nuclear Strike 'De-escalation,'" *Bulletin of the Atomic Scientists*, March 13, 2014.

———, "Bill Gertz, New Russian SLCM, and the True Nature of Challenge to US and NATO," *Arms Control Wonk Blog*, August 25, 2015. As of August 27, 2015
http://lewis.armscontrolwonk.com/archive/7801/sokov-on-russian-cruise-missiles

Spiegel Online International, "Spiegel Survey on the Crimea Crisis," TNS Forschung, March 19–20, 2014. As of August 27, 2015:
http://www.spiegel.de/international/germany/bild-961711-674691.html

Sutyagin, Igor, *Atomic Accounting: A New Estimate of Russia's Non-Strategic Nuclear Forces*, occasional paper, London: Royal United Services Institute, 2012.

Torry, Harriet, "Germans Back Tougher Stance Toward Russia over Ukraine—Poll," *Wall Street Journal*, August 8, 2014. As of August 27, 2015:
http://www.wsj.com/articles/
germans-back-tougher-stance-toward-russia-over-ukraine-poll-1407495865

"Ukraine Crisis Hampers German Carmaker's Russia Growth," *Moscow Times*, August 3, 2014.

United Nations, Comtrade Database, online database, undated. As of August 27, 2015:
http://comtrade.un.org

U.S. Department of Defense, "America's Continued Commitment to European Security: Operation Atlantic Resolve," web page, undated. As of August 27, 2015:
http://www.defense.gov/home/features/2014/0514_atlanticresolve/

U.S. European Command, Communication and Engagement Directorate, "Operational Atlantic Resolve (2014)," fact sheet, 2014. As of August 27, 2015:
http://www.defense.gov/home/features/2014/0514_atlanticresolve/
Operation_Atlantic_Resolve_Fact_Sheet_2014.pdf

VoteWatch Europe, "EU-Ukraine Association Agreement, with the Exception of the Treatment of Third Country Nationals Legally Employed as Workers in the Territory of the Other Party," September 16, 2014.

Wagstyl, Stefan, "Germany Acts to Counter Russia's Balkan Designs," *Financial Times*, November 27, 2014. As of August 27, 2015:
http://www.ft.com/cms/s/0/
5e1d833c-7659-11e4-a704-00144feabdc0.html#axzz3k31hnC3c

White House, Office of the Press Secretary, "Remarks by President Obama to the People of Estonia," speech in Tallinn, Estonia, September 3, 2014. As of August 27, 2015:
https://www.whitehouse.gov/the-press-office/2014/09/03/
remarks-president-obama-people-estonia

"Wieder Krieg in Europa? Nicht in Unserem Namen!" *Zeit* Online, December 5, 2014. As of August 27, 2015:
http://www.zeit.de/politik/2014-12/aufruf-russland-dialog

YouGov, "Survey Results," poll conducted among northwestern European adults, March 21–27, 2014. As of February 23, 2016:
http://cdn.yougov.com/cumulus_uploads/document/n1z35e9mya/
YG-Archive-140327-Ukraine-Eurotrack.pdf

Zander, Christina, and John D. Stoll, "Volvo Trucks Puts Russian Tank Deal on Ice," *Wall Street Journal*, April 8, 2014.